D1278491

MAR   2016

FRANCES T. BOURNE
JACARANDA PUBLIC LIBRARY

4143 WOODMERE PARK BLVD.
VENICE, FL 34293

31969024298357

The
Importance of
**SCIENTIFIC
THEORY**

The Importance of Plate Tectonic Theory

Peggy J. Parks

FRANCES T. BOURNE
JACARANDA PUBLIC LIBRARY
4143 WOODMERE PARK BLVD.
VENICE, FL 34293

ReferencePoint
Press®

San Diego, CA

About the Author

Peggy J. Parks holds a bachelor of science degree from Aquinas College in Grand Rapids, Michigan, where she graduated magna cum laude. An author who has written dozens of educational books on a wide variety of topics for children and young adults, Parks lives in Muskegon, Michigan, a town that she says inspires her writing because of its location on the shores of Lake Michigan.

© 2016 ReferencePoint Press, Inc.
Printed in the United States

For more information, contact:
ReferencePoint Press, Inc.
PO Box 27779
San Diego, CA 92198
www.ReferencePointPress.com

ALL RIGHTS RESERVED.
No part of this work covered by the copyright hereon may be reproduced or used in any form or by any means—graphic, electronic, or mechanical, including photocopying, recording, taping, web distribution, or information storage retrieval systems—without the written permission of the publisher.

Picture Credits:
Cover: © Jim Wark/Visuals Unlimited/Corbis; Accurate Art, Inc., 10; © Martin Alipaz/epa/Corbis, 59; © Stefano Bianchetti/Corbis, 17; © Adam Chang/Corbis, 53; Depositphotos, 6 (top, bottom left), 7 (bottom), 15, 37, 57; Dominique Gutekunst/ZUMA Press/Newscom, 49; Gary Hincks/Science Photo Library, 28; Dorling Kindersley Universal Images Group/Newscom, 23; Dr. Ken MacDonald/Science Photo Library, 26; NOAA/Science Photo Library, 63; © Danu Primanto/Demotix/Corbis, 67; Monica Schroeder/Science Source/Science Photo Library, 41; Thinkstock, 6 (bottom right), 7 (top); © Jeff Vanuga/Corbis, 45

LIBRARY OF CONGRESS CATALOGING-IN-PUBLICATION DATA

Parks, Peggy J., 1951- author.
  The importance of plate tectonic theory / by Peggy J. Parks.
    pages cm. -- (The importance of scientific theory)
  Audience: Grades 9 to 12
  Includes bibliographical references and index.
  ISBN-13: 978-1-60152-894-0 (hardback)
  ISBN-10: 1-60152-894-9 (hardback)
  1. Plate tectonics--Juvenile literature. 2. Geology, Structural--Juvenile literature. I. Title.
  QE511.4.P356 2016
  551.1'36--dc23

                                                              2015000656

CONTENTS

FOREWORD

What is the nature of science? The authors of "Understanding the Scientific Enterprise: The Nature of Science in the Next Generation Science Standards," answer that question this way: "Science is a way of explaining the natural world. In common parlance, science is both a set of practices and the historical accumulation of knowledge. An essential part of science education is learning science and engineering practices and developing knowledge of the concepts that are foundational to science disciplines. Further, students should develop an understanding of the enterprise of science as a whole—the wondering, investigating, questioning, data collecting and analyzing."

Examples from history offer a valuable way to explore the nature of science and understand the core ideas and concepts around which all life revolves. When English chemist John Dalton formulated a theory in 1803 that all matter consists of small, indivisible particles called atoms and that atoms of different elements have different properties, he was building on the ideas of earlier scientists as well as relying on his own experimentation, observation, and analysis. His atomic theory, which also proposed that atoms cannot be created or destroyed, was not entirely accurate, yet his ideas are remarkably close to the modern understanding of atoms. Intrigued by his findings, other scientists continued to test and build on Dalton's ideas until eventually—a century later—actual proof of the atom's existence emerged.

The story of these discoveries and what grew from them is presented in *The Importance of Atomic Theory*, one volume in Reference-Point's series *The Importance of Scientific Theory*. The series strives to help students develop a broader and deeper understanding of the nature of science by examining notable ideas and events in the history of science. Books in the series focus on the development and outcomes of atomic theory, cell theory, germ theory, evolution theory, plate tectonic theory, and more. All books clearly state the core idea and explore changes in thinking over time, methods of experimentation and observation, and societal impacts of these momentous theories and discoveries. Each volume includes a visual chronology; brief descriptions of important people; sidebars that highlight and further explain key events and concepts; "words in context" vocabulary; and, where possible, the words of the scientists themselves.

Through richly detailed examples from history and clear discussion of scientific ideas and methods, *The Importance of Scientific Theory* series furthers an appreciation for the essence of science and the men and women who devote their lives to it. As the authors of "Understanding the Scientific Enterprise: The Nature of Science in the Next Generation Science Standards" write, "With the addition of historical examples, the nature of scientific explanations assumes a human face and is recognized as an ever-changing enterprise."

IMPORTANT DATES IN THE HISTORY OF PLATE TECTONICS

1596
In his atlas *Thesaurus Geographicus*, Flemish geographer and cartographer Abraham Ortelius notes that the Americas look as though they were "torn away" from Europe and Africa.

1910
Johns Hopkins University geologist Harry Fielding Reid publishes a report describing elastic rebound, which is his theory of how stored energy is released and spread during an earthquake.

1858
After identical tropical plant fossils are observed in North American and European coal deposits, Italian American geographer Antonio Snider-Pellegrini suggests that the continents may have once been connected.

1922
Alfred Wegener's book *The Origin of Continents and Oceans* is published in English and four other languages; Wegener is reviled and his theory rejected and ridiculed by scientists worldwide.

1600 /	1900	1910	1920	1930

1855
Using an underwater mapping technique called bathymetry, US Navy lieutenant Matthew F. Maury discovers the first evidence of underwater mountains in the central Atlantic Ocean.

1908
American geologist Frank B. Taylor proposes that the long, curved mountain belts of Asia and Europe resulted from tidal forces of the moon pushing and pulling earth's crust, which formed carpet-like folds that built up over time.

1937
South African geologist Alexander du Toit, an avid supporter of Alfred Wegener and his continental drift theory, publishes a thesis called *Our Wandering Continents*, in which he analyzes evidence to support the theory.

1915
Alfred Wegener's *The Origin of Continents and Oceans* is published in German; in it he explains the viability of his continental drift theory and refutes other prevailing scientific beliefs.

1912
At a meeting in Germany, meteorologist Alfred Wegener presents his continental displacement (or continental drift) theory that earth's continents were once joined as a single landmass that broke apart, with separate continents "drifting" away over time to their present locations.

1963
British geologists Frederick J. Vine and Drummond Matthews describe their theory about seafloor spreading and its relationship to plate movement in a paper titled "Magnetic Anomalies over Oceanic Ridges."

2012
Upon analyzing satellite images from NASA's *THEMIS* spacecraft, University of California–Los Angeles professor of earth and space sciences An Yin discovers signs that plate tectonics exists on Mars.

1945
While on a submarine mission, US Navy commander and geologist Harry H. Hess discovers hundreds of flat-topped mountains on the floor of the Pacific Ocean, which he later calls *guyots*.

1967
British geologist Dan Peter McKenzie and American geologist Robert L. Parker publish the first scientific paper describing the principles of plate tectonics.

| 1940 | 1960 | 1980 | 2000 | 2020 |

1960
Geologist Harry H. Hess theorizes that the movement of continents results from newly formed ocean crust spreading away from mid-ocean ridges; in the process, he discovers a geological phenomenon called seafloor spreading, which is shown to play a major role in plate movement.

1977
Geologist Bruce C. Heezen and oceanographer and cartographer Marie Tharp publish the World Ocean Floor Map, the first scientific map of the entire seafloor.

2014
Based on data from NASA's *Galileo* spacecraft, scientists learn that Jupiter's icy moon Europa may have active tectonic plates similar to those of Earth.

1965
Canadian geophysicist John Tuzo-Wilson coins the term *plate* to define the massive slabs of rock that make up Earth's crust.

1968
Columbia University geologists Bryan Isacks, Jack Oliver, and Lynn R. Sykes publish a paper in which they theorize that earth's crust is broken into a number of plates that are constantly sliding around.

INTRODUCTION

A Restless Earth

THE CORE IDEA

Plate tectonics is a scientific theory that explains the formation and continuous reshaping of earth's outer shell, or lithosphere. According to this theory, the lithosphere is broken up into a few dozen massive, irregularly shaped slabs of rock called plates. The continents sit atop the plates, as do the oceans. Floating on a churning layer of partially molten rock known as the asthenosphere, the plates are constantly in motion. At the boundaries where they meet, they slide past each other, grind against each other, and sometimes violently collide. Earthquakes and volcanic eruptions are explained by the plate tectonics theory, as are the building of mountains and the formation of deep ocean trenches. Plate tectonics also explains why the coastlines of West Africa and South America look like they could fit together; because hundreds of millions of years ago they *were* together, as part of the same enormous landmass.

In 1922 scientists throughout the world were shocked and outraged to hear of a new scientific theory called continental drift. The theory was developed by Alfred Wegener, a meteorologist from Berlin, Germany. After studying scientific papers and world maps, Wegener had become convinced that the continents were once a single landmass—a supercontinent that he called Pangaea (from the Greek words meaning "all land"). Wegener's reasoning was that over time, and due to unknown forces, the continents had broken away from the landmass and slowly drifted to their current locations.

A number of factors played a role in Wegener's conclusion, and one of the most compelling was the peculiar distribution of fossils. During his studies of the scientific research, he learned that the fossilized remains of similar (and sometimes identical) plants and animals had been found near the east coast of South America and the west coast of Africa. Today these continents are separated by the vast Atlantic Ocean and have very different ecosystems—but Wegener believed that was not always the case. He became convinced that the continents had once been connected.

Another piece of evidence that there was once a single landmass was the shape of the coastlines. Wegener had long been intrigued by this, thinking that the continents resembled gigantic puzzle pieces that were made to fit together. In a December 1910 letter to his future wife, Else Köppen, he wrote: "Doesn't the east coast of South America fit exactly against the west coast of Africa, as if they had once been joined? This is an idea I'll have to pursue."[1]

Relentless Scorn

Wegener first presented his theory in January 1912 at an annual meeting of the Geological Association in Frankfurt, Germany. Other than raising some eyebrows among the scientists in attendance, the theory garnered little attention. Awareness was also low after the release of Wegener's 1915 book, *The Origin of Continents and Oceans*, which was initially published only in German. But seven years later, when the book became available in English and four other languages, news of the Wegener's theory raced through the scientific world. This, says *Smithsonian* magazine's Richard Conniff, was when "the international fireworks exploded."[2]

WORDS IN CONTEXT

tectonics
The formation and structure of the earth's lithosphere.

What came to be known as the continental drift theory was denounced by geologists worldwide, with some of the most vicious attacks coming from the United States. During a presentation at a 1926 meeting, influential University of Chicago geologist Rollin Thomas Chamberlin dismissed the notion of moving continents by issuing a challenge to his colleagues: "Can we call geology a science when there exists such difference of opinion on fundamental matters as to make it possible for such a theory . . . to run wild?"[3]

Undaunted by the widespread scorn and rejection, Wegener remained certain that his continental drift theory was correct—but

The Internal Structure of Earth

The earth consists of three main layers: crust, mantle, and core. The outermost layer, the crust, is thin and brittle. The middle layer, the mantle, is a dense, hot layer of semi-solid rock. Beneath the mantle, at the center of the earth, lies the core. It is nearly twice as dense as the mantle. The core consists of two distinct parts: a liquid outer core and a solid inner core. The crust and uppermost part of the mantle together form a rigid layer of rock called the lithosphere. This is where the earth's moving plates are found. Scientists believe that a narrow zone of hot, semi-solid material exists below the lithosphere. They call this zone the asthenosphere. Over geologic time the asthenosphere is subjected to extreme pressure and high temperatures, causing it to soften and flow. Scientists believe that the rigid lithosphere moves, or floats, on the slowly flowing asthenosphere.

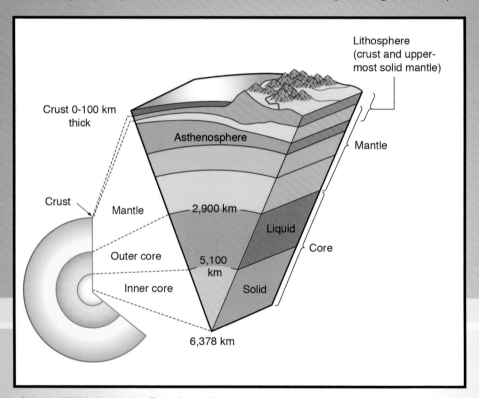

Source: USGS, "Inside the Earth." http://pubs.usgs.gov.

he never succeeded in convincing his fellow scientists. By the time he died in 1930, the theory had all but faded into obscurity. "Geologists largely chose to forget Alfred Wegener," says Conniff, "except to launch another flurry of attacks on his 'fairy tale' theory in the middle of World War II." He adds that it was customary for older geologists to warn newcomers to the field "that any hint of an interest in continental drift would doom their careers."[4]

An Era of Discovery

Things began to change during the 1950s and the 1960s. For the first time ever, scientists were exploring the ocean depths, and they found evidence on the seafloor that pointed toward continental drift as a viable theory. This was a time when scientists welcomed and embraced new theories about the earth, rather than merely clinging to existing beliefs. In a 1970 paper, the late geologist Francis J. Pettijohn described a renewed interest in earth sciences, meteorology, and oceanography. He said the result of this scientific enthusiasm was to "infuse new life, new techniques, new ideas into a discipline grown old." According to Pettijohn, technology and sophisticated exploratory tools "awakened new interest in continental drift."[5] As more and more scientists embraced the theory, they acknowledged that Wegener had been correct all along—the continents were indeed mobile, rather than stationary. The widespread acceptance of this concept profoundly changed the study of geology and became the forerunner to the theory of plate tectonics.

> **WORDS IN CONTEXT**
>
> *plate*
> An enormous, rigid slab of solid rock.

Geologist Adam T. Mansur refers to plate tectonics as "the elegant theory that shapes how geologists understand the Earth's surface."[6] The word *tectonics* is derived from the Greek word *tektonikos*, which pertains to building or construction. In the field of geology, *tectonics* refers to the formation and structure of earth's lithosphere, which is composed of the crust and upper mantle. Geologists have concluded that the lithosphere is broken into massive, rigid slabs of rock called plates; hence the term *plate tectonics*.

Development of the plate tectonics theory was a collective effort, with scientists from the United States, Britain, and Canada all playing important roles. With each new discovery, from seafloor spreading and oceanic ridges to variations in earth's magnetic field over time, scientific understanding of the earth has grown substantially. The plate tectonics theory has provided answers to questions scientists struggled with for centuries, such as why earthquakes occur in specific areas; how volcanoes were formed and what causes them to erupt; and how mountain ranges such as the towering Alps in Europe and the highest mountains in the world, the mighty Himalayas, were built over time. "In short," says British scientist Roy Livermore, "plate tectonics explains at a stroke all the important geological phenomena on Earth."[7]

WORDS IN CONTEXT

lithosphere

The outer shell of the earth, composed of the upper mantle and crust.

As technology has increasingly grown more sophisticated, scientists have continued to expand their knowledge of plate tectonics. There is every reason to believe that this scientific understanding will continue to expand and more fascinating discoveries about the ever-changing earth will be made in the future.

CHAPTER ONE

Early Scientific Beliefs

Throughout history the earth and how it was formed have been topics of interest and fascination for scientists worldwide. From the planet's vast oceans to towering mountain ranges and deep, wide canyons, mysteries abound. In the publication *This Dynamic Earth: The Story of Plate Tectonics*, authors Jacquelyne Kious and Robert I. Tilling write: "Why is the Earth so restless? What causes the ground to shake violently, volcanoes to erupt with explosive force, and great mountain ranges to rise to incredible heights? Scientists, philosophers, and theologians have wrestled with questions such as these for centuries."[8]

The widely accepted belief among early scientists was that earth's continents had always been in the same fixed positions. This perspective was rarely questioned, although a few scientists strayed from it. One of the first to question the fixed-earth philosophy was Abraham Ortelius, a Flemish geographer and cartographer (mapmaker) who lived during the sixteenth century. After illustrating hundreds of maps, Ortelius had become very familiar with the continents and how they were shaped. During the course of his work, he made a surprising discovery: the coastlines of Africa and what is now known as South America looked like they were made to fit together. If that were true, Ortelius reasoned, it meant that some powerful force had caused the landmass to break apart and change positions. More than three hundred years before Alfred Wegener proposed that the continents were mobile rather than fixed in place, Ortelius had arrived at much the same conclusion.

> **WORDS IN CONTEXT**
>
> *cartographer*
> A person whose specialty is creating maps.

Observations of an Ancient Cartographer

In 1570, based on information he had gathered about seagoing expeditions, Ortelius published a comprehensive book of maps known as an atlas. The book, which was titled *Theatrum Orbis Terrarum* (*Theater of the World*), featured seventy double-page world maps along with meticulously detailed historical narratives and source references. Because of its beautiful illustrations and encyclopedic descriptions, Ortelius's *Theatrum* was unlike any collection of maps ever created before. Marcel van den Broecke, an expert on ancient cartography, describes *Theatrum* this way: "It was the first modern world atlas in the sense of a collection of uniformly-sized maps covering the contemporary world, each backed with text, put together to form a coherent book. The *Theatrum* was immensely popular."[9]

Ortelius published many revised editions of his atlas in the years following release of the first volume, selling an estimated seventy-three hundred copies. One expanded edition, titled *Thesaurus Geographicus*, was published in 1596. Like the other versions, this one featured a large collection of world maps along with detailed descriptions and references pertaining to each. What was unique about *Thesaurus*, though, was that for the first time in his narrative Ortelius pointed out the puzzle-like shape of the continents' coastlines. He described the Americas (often known during this era as, simply, *America*) as appearing to have been "torn away from Europe and Africa," which he inferred was caused by floods and earthquakes. As evidence for his claim that the continents had once been connected, Ortelius wrote that "vestiges of the rupture reveal themselves, if someone brings forward a map of the world and considers carefully the coasts of the three aforementioned parts of the earth, where they face each other—I mean the projecting parts of Europe and Africa, of course, along with the recesses of America."[10]

> **WORDS IN CONTEXT**
>
> *catastrophism*
>
> A philosophy in which changes in the earth over time are primarily attributed to sudden violent events.

Catastrophism

Nearly three centuries passed before Ortelius's theory about the continents became a topic of serious interest for scientists worldwide.

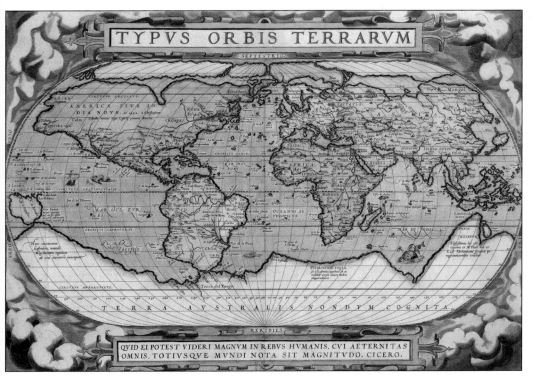

TYPVS ORBIS TERRARVM

Flemish cartographer Abraham Ortelius published a remarkable world atlas in 1570. Maps such as this one (reproduced from his atlas), led Ortelius to believe that the Americas had once been attached to and then torn away from Europe and Africa.

In the 1850s Antonio Snider-Pellegrini, an Italian American geographer living in Paris, France, became curious about why the coastlines looked like gigantic puzzle pieces. Also, like a growing number of scientists, Snider-Pellegrini was fascinated to learn that fossils of the same plant and animal species had been found on continents now separated by the Atlantic Ocean. Science historian Naomi Oreskes refers to the "striking similarities" of plant and animal fossils that were discovered in parts of India, Africa, and South America. "Indeed," says Oreskes, "in some cases the fossils seemed to be identical, even though they were found thousands of miles apart. . . . If plants and animals had evolved independently in different places within diverse environments, then why did they look so similar?"[11] As Snider-Pellegrini viewed it, there could be only one explanation: At one time the continents must have been a single landmass.

In 1859 Snider-Pellegrini published a book called *La création et ses mystères dévoilés* (*Creation and Its Mysteries Unveiled*). The book included two maps: one showing separate continents divided by the Atlantic

The Atlas Maker

History has shown that Abraham Ortelius was one of the first people to observe the shape of earth's continents; specifically, that they looked like pieces of a giant jigsaw puzzle. During the sixteenth century, Ortelius made his living as a professional illuminator, meaning an artist who used gold and silver leaf in creating illustrations. His specialty was maps, and he illustrated hundreds of them during the mid-sixteenth century. But it was not until 1570, with the publication of the world's first true atlas, called *Theatrum Orbis Terrarum* (*Theater of the World*), that Ortelius became rich and famous. The Library of Congress explains: "It was the *Theatrum* that firmly established his reputation as a cartographer and made him a wealthy man."

From *Theatrum*'s publication in 1570 until 1612, Ortelius revised and expanded the atlas thirty-one times. It was his 1596 edition, titled *Thesaurus Geographicus*, in which he noted that the coastlines of Africa and South America looked as though they had once been joined and at some point were ripped apart.

Library of Congress, "Ortelius Atlas." http://memory.loc.gov.

Ocean, and the other showing how the continents might have looked as a single landmass. Norwegian geologist Allan Krill describes these as a "a set of two dramatic globe maps indicating that the Atlantic Ocean had formed when a continent had broken up and separated. On these maps, South America is labeled as *Atlantide* or the lost continent Atlantis. Australia was originally connected to western Africa, so all continents (except the relatively unknown Antarctica) were once united."[12]

Although Snider-Pellegrini relied on scientific evidence and logic when formulating his theories about the continents, his beliefs were also deeply rooted in biblical teachings. He subscribed to a theory known as catastrophism, in which changes in the earth over time are primarily attributed to sudden violent events such as earthquakes and floods. As a devout Christian, Snider-Pellegrini theorized that an ancient single continent had been violently ripped apart by the catastrophic flood chronicled in the Bible's book of Genesis. He suspected that because the earth was "lopsided," with all the land concentrated in one massive continent on one hemisphere, the flood could have been a way of restoring the planet's balance. Australian geologist Samuel Warren Carey describes Snider-Pellegrini's version of catastrophism:

> This lopsided arrangement had broken up during the biblical flood, with the Americas drifting westward, opening the Atlantic with its complementary coastlines. The whole book is a grand elaboration of the six "days" of *Genesis*. The Moon was expelled during the convulsions of the first "day." The fifth "day" produced Pangaea and the complementary primordial ocean. Noah's flood and the disruption of Pangaea occurred during the sixth "day."[13]

Geographer Antonio Snider-Pellegrini believed that the earth once held a single massive continent that was ripped apart by the catastrophic biblical flood (depicted in artwork from the 1800s). This idea found few supporters in the scientific community.

Earth Like an Apple

Snider-Pellegrini's theory about the catastrophic flood was not accepted by most scientists, but like him, many wondered about the shape of the continents' coastlines. British scientist John R. Gribbin explains: "A few people took on board Snider-Pellegrini's idea that South America and Africa had split apart from a single landmass, while quietly ignoring his suggestion that this happened all at once, in a sudden catastrophe."[14] Another lingering scientific mystery was the matter of identical fossils on separate continents, for which no one could come up with a reasonable explanation.

Also puzzling to scientists during the mid- to late 1800s was the origin of the world's mountains. Geologists worldwide puzzled over how diverse types of mountain ranges had formed and, as Oreskes asks, what kind of massive force could have possibly "squeezed and folded rocks like putty?"[15] At the time a common hypothesis for mountain building was known as the contracting earth theory, or contraction theory. The premise was that the earth was once a molten ball; in the process of cooling, its surface cracked and folded up on itself. "It was widely believed that Earth had formed as a hot, incandescent body," says Oreskes, "and had been steadily cooling since the beginning of geological time. Because most materials contract as they cool, it seemed logical to assume that Earth had been contracting as it cooled, too. As it did, its surface would have deformed, producing mountains."[16]

One of the leading proponents of the contracting earth theory was Austrian geologist Edward Suess, who popularized the metaphorical image of earth as a drying apple. According to Suess, as the planet cooled and contracted, it wrinkled to accommodate the shrinking surface area. Over millions of years, these "wrinkles" grew into mountains, as scientists Michael J. Smith and John B. Southard explain: "Suess stated that, as the Earth cooled from a molten state, the more dense materials contracted and sank toward the center, and the least dense materials 'floated' and cooled to form the crust. He then speculated that mountain ranges formed from the contraction and cooling of the Earth. He likened this to the way that an apple wrinkles and folds as it dries out and shrinks."[17] Suess wrote in detail about the formation of mountains in his 1857 book, *Die Entstehung der Alpen* (*The Origin of the Alps*).

Suess was convinced that the contracting earth theory explained not only the formation of mountain ranges, but also the origin of oceans. He believed that the continents and oceans had changed positions over time. "In his model," Smith and Southard explain, "during the cooling process, parts of the Earth sank deeper than others, forming the ocean basins. Suess claimed that certain parts of the sea floor and continents could rise and sink as they adjusted to changes in the cooling Earth."[18]

Based on the premise of continents rising and sinking over time, Suess proposed that there had once been huge land bridges that connected continents separated by vast expanses of ocean. This, he believed, could explain the existence of similar or even identical fossils on continents that are now separated by oceans. Smith and Southard write: "According to Suess, the land bridges allowed various animals and plants to spread without crossing an ocean."[19] Suess and other like-minded scientists believed that at some point in history, the land bridges had simply sunk to the bottom of the ocean.

WORDS IN CONTEXT

land bridges

Continent-sized landmasses (now known to be nonexistent) that some nineteenth-century geologists believed had once connected the continents.

Permanence Theory

Suess's contracting earth theory became a popular topic of discussion among scientists during the mid-1800s, with some in Europe endorsing it. Scientists in North America, however, tended toward the beliefs of James Dwight Dana, a geologist from Utica, New York. Dana developed his own version of the contracting earth theory. Like Suess, he believed that the earth had once been a molten ball that had cooled and contracted over time. Beyond that, however, Dana's beliefs differed in a number of ways. For instance, he did not believe that the continents had moved; rather, he was convinced that they had stayed in roughly the same positions since being formed early in the planet's history. Also unlike Suess, Dana believed that the oceans were fixed in place and had not changed throughout time. He subscribed to a philosophy that was popular among like-minded scientists: "Once a continent, always a continent; once an ocean, always an ocean."[20]

Dana's version of the contracting earth theory came to be called permanence theory, as Oreskes writes: "Although clearly a type of contraction theory, resting as it did on the premise of global cooling, Dana's work was perceived by his American colleagues as standing in opposition to the 'contraction' hypothesis articulated by Suess. Although starting from the same premise, Suess and Dana had come to very different conclusions about the present state of the globe."[21]

By the latter half of the nineteenth century, field research and mathematical analyses had begun to show that any form of contracting earth theory was deeply flawed. The fundamental problem with both Suess's and Dana's versions, says geologist Adam T. Mansur, was that planetary contraction "could produce neither the pattern nor extent of deformation seen in existing mountain belts."[22] Detailed mapping of Europe's great Alps mountain range and the Appalachians in North America had shown that the high elevations could not have resulted from a cooling earth. Rather, they had formed when huge sections of continental crust had been compressed over geological time. Mansur explains: "Thermal contraction was unable to account for such large amounts of compression." Evidence continued to mount, and by the early twentieth century any notion of a contracting earth had been discredited. "The need for new explanations was evident and growing,"[23] says Mansur.

WORDS IN CONTEXT

paleontologic
Related to paleontology, a branch of science that involves studying fossils.

Accepted at Last

Despite the flaws and inconsistencies found in many proposed theories, the research by early scientists was invaluable to Alfred Wegener. In 1911, while at the University of Marburg in Germany, he came upon a scientific paper that summarized the paleontologic (related to fossils) evidence for an ancient land bridge between Africa and Brazil. The paper cited similarities between specific rock strata, as well as the fossilized remains of plants and animals encased in rock, all of which had been observed on opposite sides of the Atlantic Ocean. Wegener was intrigued by the information contained in the paper,

Compelling Evidence

In developing his continental drift theory, Alfred Wegener concluded that several hundred million years ago the earth had been a single landmass. He was influenced by scientists who had observed the fossilized remains of identical plants and animals on separate continents. NASA science writer Patrick Hughes explains: "Wegener believed this fact was one of the strongest pieces of evidence for his theory."

One creature whose fossilized remains were found on the South American and African continents was a land reptile known as *Cynognathus*. The reptile, which was nearly 9 feet (2.7 m) long, lived during the Triassic period, between 200 million and 250 million years ago. A smaller land reptile, known as the *Lystrosaurus*, lived in the regions that are now Antarctica, India, and South America. An aquatic creature from the same era was the *Mesosaurus*, which was a long, thin reptile that lived in freshwater lakes and ponds. *Mesosaurus* fossils were found in the southernmost part of South America and Africa. Fossilized remains of a fern known as the *Glossopteris* have been observed in all continents in the Southern Hemisphere, including South America, the southern part of Africa, Antarctica, and Australia. "Certain fossils appear in continuous bands across continents that are now separated by thousands of miles of ocean," says Hughes.

Patrick Hughes, "Alfred Wegener (1880–1930)," NASA Earth Observatory. http://earthobservatory.nasa.gov.

although he found the notion of land bridges to be far-fetched. He had serious doubts about whether such slabs of land could sink and remain at the bottom of the ocean. At the time, according to British scientist John R. Gribbin, it was widely known among scientists that the rocks of the seafloor were denser, meaning more closely compacted and heavier, than rocks of the continental crust. He writes:

> Continents are like icebergs floating in the denser material beneath the crust. If some mysterious force had made continental land bridges sink into the underlying material, they should have bobbed up again, just as an ice cube pushed below the surface of a glass of water will bob back up. And Wegener

knew a thing or two about the behaviour of floating ice, because he had worked as an official meteorologist on a Danish expedition to Greenland. Floating ice cannot sink beneath the waves—but floating ice sheets can break up and drift apart, with the watery gaps between them widening.[24]

Wegener's interest in early scientific observations continued to grow. He began to seek out and study additional research about fossil discoveries, along with closely scrutinizing world maps. He remained convinced that land bridges never existed, but he could not disregard the complementary coastlines of Africa and South America. He often wondered, why did they look like pieces of a gigantic jigsaw puzzle? The idea of a single landmass that had split apart began taking root in his mind—although for that to be true meant the continents had moved, and this conflicted with prevailing views of the time. Says Australian geologist Andrew Gleadow:

> To argue that the continents were once part of a single landmass required that Wegener abandon the assumption that relative positions of the continents were fixed. This did not trouble him. He argued that the continents were like great ships moving through plastic material of the ocean crust. If the continents could move, he reasoned, their present positions did not conflict with the previous existence of Pangaea.[25]

By 1912 Wegener had the first version of his continental drift theory ready to present. Time after time, however, he and his ideas were rejected by other scientists. Although Wegener continued to make adjustments to the theory over the following years, few people believed there was any validity to it. "For many critics," says Gleadow, "the argument against continental drift boiled down to a single point: Continents could not move."[26] Wegener, however, knew those critics were wrong, and right up until his death in 1930, he never stopped believing in the theory of continental drift.

By the mid-1950s, two decades after Wegener's death, a growing number of scientists were starting to understand the logic of his ideas. NASA science writer Patrick Hughes explains: "A series of confirm-

To Alfred Wegener, the world's continents resembled a giant jigsaw puzzle whose parts had once been joined and then split apart. He realized that this meant something unthinkable for the time: that continents could move.

ing discoveries in paleomagnetism and oceanography finally convinced most scientists that continents do indeed move. Moreover, as Wegener had predicted, the movement is part of a grandscale process that causes mountain-building, earthquakes, volcanic eruptions, sea-level fluctuations, and apparent polar wandering as it rearranges Earth's geography." The "grandscale process" to which Hughes refers is plate tectonics, a theory that has completely revolutionized the study of geology—and vindicated Wegener. "During the last few decades," says Hughes, "Alfred Wegener has finally gotten the recognition he deserves. Unfortunately, as with most visionaries, it must be posthumous praise."[27]

CHAPTER TWO

Development of the Plate Tectonics Theory

Throughout the late 1950s and early 1960s, as one scientist after another embraced the theory of continental drift, some remained staunchly opposed to it. One of the most adamant objectors to the theory was Sir Harold Jeffreys, a distinguished and highly respected British geophysicist and professor at England's renowned Cambridge University. Jeffreys denounced any and all viewpoints of scientists who sought to prove that continents were mobile and had changed positions over time. Whenever he encountered that perspective, Jeffreys explained that the earth was rigid and solid, which he said had been shown through seismic wave studies. Therefore, he went on to emphasize, continental movement was physically impossible. "In essence," says the late geophysicist Gordon J.F. MacDonald, "[Jeffreys] argued that the earth was too strong to permit significant crustal mobility. It was rigid, not flexible."[28] Jeffreys continued to stand by his assertion that the earth was solid, rigid, and immobile. Because of his credibility, along with the lack of irrefutable proof that continents had moved over time, many scientists shared his views. As the years went by, however, that number dwindled.

A Time of Discovery

By the early 1960s the continents had been mapped extensively, but the same was not true of the ocean floor. "It was nonetheless clear," says MacDonald, "that volcanic activity, with massive flows of liquid lava, had taken place in the ocean basin." Given the amount of volcanic activity on the ocean floor, even skeptical geologists began to think that maybe the earth was not so rigid and unmoving after all. MacDonald, a longtime supporter of Jeffreys, began to question whether only the ocean floor was mobile whereas the continents remained fixed. "Perhaps the sea floor moved without displacing the continents?," he suggested. MacDonald adds that during the early 1960s new scientific findings and interpretations of ocean floor data led to the theory of plate tectonics, which he says "permanently altered the discussions of the mobility of the earth."[29]

One geologist who played a major role in clearing up the mystery of continental mobility was Harry H. Hess. During World War II, when Hess was serving as an admiral with the US Navy, he commanded an attack transport ship called the USS *Cape Johnson*. A Princeton University geology professor, Hess was fascinated with the ocean floor because so little was known about it. His ship was equipped with an instrument known as a deep-sea fathometer (or echo sounder). This device used sound waves to determine the depth of the water below the ship's bottom as well as detect objects in the water or on the ocean floor. As the *Cape Johnson* cruised through the Pacific Ocean from one battle to the next, Hess kept the sounding equipment running day and night. This allowed him to gather depth and topographic data on thousands of miles of ocean floor.

Hess was particularly intrigued by his discovery that the seafloor was studded with several hundred peculiar flat-topped mountains. He was puzzled by their flattened tops, which looked as though the mountains had been sheared off or eroded. But since they were thousands of feet beneath the surface of the water, Hess had no idea how such erosion would be possible. He named the flat-topped mountains "guyots" in honor of Swiss geologist Arnold H. Guyot. In the mid-nineteenth century Guyot had founded Princeton's geology department, where Hess had been a professor before joining the war effort.

WORDS IN CONTEXT

guyots
Flat-topped mountains located on the ocean floor.

Answers from the Ocean Depths

Hess returned to Princeton after the war ended, and over the following years he devoted much of his time to studying the ocean floor. A number of other geologists were also aggressively pursuing this

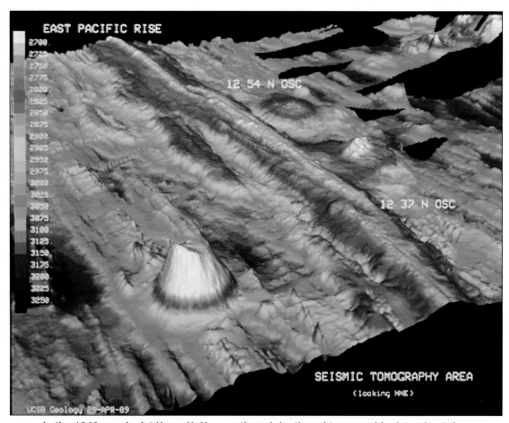

In the 1940s geologist Harry H. Hess gathered depth and topographic data about the ocean floor. A more recent topographic map of the Pacific Ocean seafloor reveals various formations including a mid-ocean ridge (red) that runs northward from near Antarctica to the Gulf of California.

research, as American Museum of Natural History curator Edmond A. Mathez explains: "The postwar period was a revolutionary one for the earth sciences. Efforts to map the ocean floor intensified, thanks in large part to the newly-created US Office of Naval Research. Within a few years, a curious terrain had emerged: vast, flat plains interrupted by ridges, or more precisely, vast mountain ranges."[30]

The "ridges" to which Mathez refers are collectively known as the global mid-ocean ridge, an immense underwater mountain chain that extends through the world's major oceans. The Mid-Atlantic Ridge, for instance, cuts through the Arctic and Atlantic oceans. Earth's longest mountain range, the mid-ocean ridge stretches for more than 40,300 miles (64,857 km) and in some areas is more than 900 miles

(1,448 km) wide. In the publication *This Dynamic Earth: The Story of Plate Tectonics*, authors Jacquelyne Kious and Robert I. Tilling explain that the ridge "zig-zags between the continents, winding its way around the globe like the seam on a baseball." Kious and Tilling go on to say that the ridge rises to an average of 14,800 feet (4,511 m) above the seafloor—higher than any other mountain in the United States except for Alaska's Mount McKinley. They write: "Though hidden beneath the ocean surface, the global mid-ocean ridge system is the most prominent topographic feature on the surface of our planet."[31]

In 1953 scientists discovered another geological wonder on the ocean floor: the Great Global Rift. This is a collection of deep canyons that run along the mid-ocean ridge system, "splitting them as though they had been sliced with a giant's knife," says Tufts University professor Kenneth R. Lang. He continues, "Hot magma emerges from beneath the sea floor, and oozes into the canyons of the Great Global Rift, filling them with lava. As the lava cools in the ocean water, it expands and pushes the ocean crust away [from] the ridge. More lava then fills the widening crack, creating new sea floor that moves laterally away from the ridge on both sides, with bilateral symmetry."[32]

WORDS IN CONTEXT

Great Global Rift

A collection of deep canyons that run along the mid-ocean ridge system.

Seafloor Spreading

These discoveries about the ocean floor were of great interest to Hess. He began to reexamine all the data he had collected during his wartime exploration, as well as research that other geologists had accumulated on the mid-ocean ridge and Great Global Rift. His motivation was finding answers to the remaining questions about the ocean floor. Referring to these as "geological puzzles," Mathez writes, "If the oceans have existed for at least 4 billion years, why has so little sediment accumulated on the ocean floor? Why are fossils found in ocean sediments no more than 180 million years old? And how do the continents move?"[33]

In 1960 Hess proposed a groundbreaking concept that helped answer these questions—and resurrected the continental drift theory that had been so widely denounced by scientists. Through his research, Hess found that the layer of sediment on most sea bottoms was surprisingly

Seafloor Spreading

New oceanic crust is created during seafloor spreading, a process that takes place over millions of years. During this process tectonic plates split apart at mid-ocean ridges, which are large mountain ranges that rise from the ocean floor. As the plates separate, hot magma wells up from the earth's mantle. Seawater then cools the magma at the edge of the plates, forming new rock. In this way, seafloor spreading creates new sections of the earth's oceanic crust.

thin. This led him to conclude that there was a vast difference in age between oceanic and continental crust, with the latter significantly older. Thus, the only plausible explanation was that the ocean floor was continuously being destroyed while new oceanic crust was being created. Hess also reasoned that if earth's crust was expanding along oceanic ridges, it had to be shrinking elsewhere. Kious and Tilling write:

> He suggested that new oceanic crust continuously spread away from the ridges in a conveyor belt–like motion. Many millions of years later, the oceanic crust eventually descends into the oceanic *trenches*—very deep, narrow canyons along the rim

of the Pacific Ocean basin. According to Hess, the Atlantic Ocean was expanding while the Pacific Ocean was shrinking. As old oceanic crust was consumed in the trenches, new magma [molten rock] rose and erupted along the spreading ridges to form new crust. In effect, the ocean basins were perpetually being "recycled," with the creation of new crust and the destruction of old oceanic lithosphere occurring simultaneously. Thus, Hess' ideas neatly explained why the Earth does not get bigger with sea floor spreading, why there is so little sediment accumulation on the ocean floor, and why oceanic rocks are much younger than continental rocks.[34]

Hess's paper about the spreading seafloor was titled "History of Ocean Basins" and was published by the Geological Society of America in 1962. Hess was well aware that his concept was a radical departure from the prevailing beliefs of most geologists. Yet he was also convinced that scientific knowledge of the oceans was at best vague and at worst erroneous. "The birth of the oceans is a matter of conjecture," Hess wrote, "the subsequent history is obscure, and the present structure is just beginning to be understood. Fascinating speculation on these subjects has been plentiful, but not much of it predating the last decade holds water." Before he went on to explain his theory about the ocean floor, Hess admitted that his beliefs might be considered fanciful by some of his

> **WORDS IN CONTEXT**
>
> *seafloor spreading*
>
> A theory in which new oceanic crust continuously spreads away from the ridges in a conveyor belt–like motion while old crust is destroyed.

peers. "I shall consider this paper an essay in geopoetry," he said. "In order not to travel any further into the realm of fantasy than is absolutely necessary I shall hold as closely as possible to a uniformitarian approach."[35] Hess was referring to the scientific theory known as uniformitarianism, which held that geological processes from the present are the same processes that occurred during the past. He was distancing himself from catastrophism, in which changes in the earth over time are attributed to sudden violent events.

Independently from Hess, an American geologist named Robert Sinclair Dietz also pursued ocean floor research during the mid-twentieth century. In fact, it was Dietz who coined the term *seafloor spreading* to describe his own theory, which was very similar to Hess's. He discussed the theory in his 1961 article "Continent and Ocean Basin Evolution by Spreading of the Sea Floor." J.I. Merritt, who authored a September 1979 Princeton University publication about Hess and other plate tectonics pioneers, explains that even though Alfred Wegener was the creator of the continental drift theory decades earlier,

> no satisfactory mechanism for explaining the drift had been found. Both Hess and Dietz proposed convection—the circular movement of a heated substance, like hot air rising in a room—as the driving force. Elaborating on an idea put forth years earlier . . . Hess suggested that the earth's mantle (the hot, dense layer of rock lying beneath the crust) had a certain plasticity that under extreme heat and pressure allowed it to move.[36]

WORDS IN CONTEXT

magma

Molten rock from deep within the earth's interior that may reach the surface through cracks in the mantle or through the eruption of volcanoes.

With the work of Hess, Dietz, and a host of other geologists, significant progress was made toward scientific understanding of the continents and oceans by the early 1960s. Still, definitive proof was missing. "Like Wegener before them," says Andrew Gleadow, "Hess and Dietz were unable to prove their new theory." Gleadow goes on to say that two scientists, University of Cambridge PhD student Frederick J. Vine and his supervisor, Drummond Matthews, finally found the evidence that had long been missing: the ocean floor magnetic stripes. "Just as Dietz and Hess surmised," says Gleadow, "new ocean floor was continually being created from molten magma and moving away from the ridges like a slow-motion conveyer belt. As the magma cooled to form new basalt rocks, they would take on the magnetic signature of Earth's field at that time."[37]

A Scientific Snub

In September 1963 the prestigious scientific journal *Nature* published a paper called "Magnetic Anomalies over Oceanic Ridges." Written by University of Cambridge PhD student Frederick J. Vine and his supervisor, Drummond Matthews, the paper discussed the concept of seafloor spreading and stated that a permanent record of continental drift could be found on the seafloor in the form of magnetic striping. The theory was hailed by scientists worldwide—but actually, three scientists should have been credited with the discovery, rather than two. The third was Canadian geologist Lawrence W. Morley, who separately came up with the same theory as Vine and Matthews but who received very different treatment.

In February 1963 Morley submitted his paper to *Nature*, but the editors rejected it, saying that there was no room to print it. He then sent the paper to another publication, the *Journal of Geophysical Research*. Months passed before he heard from the editor, who finally wrote back and gave a snide explanation for why he was rejecting Morley's work. "Such speculation makes interesting talk at cocktail parties," the editor said, "but it is not the sort of thing that ought to be published under serious scientific aegis." After the Vine-Matthews paper appeared in *Nature* and their theory was widely accepted, many scientists also gave credit to Morley. Even though his paper was never published, the theory he helped develop is often called the Vine-Matthews-Morley hypothesis of seafloor spreading.

Quoted in James Lawrence Powell, *Mysteries of Terra Firma: The Age and Evolution of the Earth.* New York: Free Press, pp. 131–32.

A Brilliant Hypothesis

Vine and Matthews expanded on the spreading seafloor hypothesis by discovering that the ocean floor was laid out in a striped magnetic pattern. They also observed that the planet's magnetism had changed direction over time. "For unknown reasons," says Merritt, "the earth has periodically reversed its magnetic polarity. When lava cools and solidifies, it 'locks in' the magnetic lines of force in effect at the time. Magma extruded along mid-ocean ridges, therefore, should record the earth's polar flip-flops like a moving film strip."[38]

In their paper, "Magnetic Anomalies over Oceanic Ridges," which was published in the September 7, 1963, issue of *Nature*, Vine and Matthews described their theory: that the ocean floor was laid out in a striped magnetic pattern that served as a permanent record of continental movement. In a more recent publication, Vine refers to the 1963 paper as "a rider to the concept of sea floor spreading, which had been proposed by Harry Hess."[39] Vine goes on to acknowledge Hess's theory that "conveyor belts" of crust and upper mantle move symmetrically away from mid-ocean ridges and passively drift continents apart. In the same publication, Vine provides details about how he and Matthews arrived at the theory that came to be known as the Vine-Matthews hypothesis. Scientists widely agree that this was the catalyst for the plate tectonics revolution. "By solving the mystery of magnetic reversals on the sea floor, Matthews and Vine found the critical last piece of the puzzle," says Gleadow. He writes:

> The spreading sea floor was now a reality. It was part of a system that recycled the sea floor in and out of the mantle beneath, and that ultimately provided the force that would explain the movement of continents. . . . After nearly 40 years of being all but banished from respectable debate, continental drift was now back on the table. . . . There was now a mechanism to explain it: sea-floor spreading. Over the next five years or so, sea-floor spreading and continental drift were combined into the grand synthesis now known as plate tectonics.[40]

The Unifying Theory

A remarkable number of geologic discoveries were made in the decades following World War II, from enormous mountain ranges on the ocean floor to the global mid-ocean ridge, Great Global Rift, and seafloor spreading. Yet scientists still remained puzzled about how all the various geological phenomena worked together. *New York Times* science journalist Kenneth Chang writes: "The space age had already begun, the first computers were crunching numbers, and yet many, if not most, earth scientists thought the continents were stuck, unmoving on the surface of the Earth."[41]

As it turned out, the answer to this scientific riddle was the theory of plate tectonics. It tied everything together, providing the unification that had long been missing. "Most of the really great breakthroughs in science are unifications," says Harvard University science historian Owen J. Gingerich. "Plate tectonics was an enormous unifying theory that began to make sense of disparate sorts of phenomena."[42]

Three Columbia University geologists, Bryan Isacks, Jack Oliver, and Lynn R. Sykes, are credited with developing a theory that they first called the "new global tectonics." In a September 1968 paper published in the *Journal of Geophysical Research*, they explained that their theory was based on the "observations of seismology," meaning

Clues from a Quake

On April 18, 1906, just after five o'clock in the morning, a catastrophic earthquake struck San Francisco and the coast of Northern California. Although the shaking only lasted for about sixty seconds, it devastated the city. An estimated three thousand people died in the quake and resulting fires, and more than half of San Francisco's 400,000 residents were left homeless. The 1906 earthquake came to be known as one of the worst natural disasters in US history.

During an investigation following the earthquake, a geologist named Harry Fielding Reid concluded that the earthquake must have resulted from an "elastic rebound" of previously stored elastic stress. The US Geological Survey (USGS) explains:

> If a stretched rubber band is broken or cut, elastic energy stored in the rubber band during the stretching will suddenly be released. Similarly, the crust of the earth can gradually store elastic stress that is released suddenly during an earthquake. This gradual accumulation and release of stress and strain is now referred to as the "elastic rebound theory" of earthquakes. Most earthquakes are the result of the sudden elastic rebound of previously stored energy.

US Geological Survey, "Reid's Elastic Rebound Theory," July 18, 2012. http://earthquake.usgs.gov.

the study of earthquakes. They also explained that the earth was broken into "a few large mobile plates of lithosphere that spread apart at ocean ridges where new surficial [relating to earth's surface] materials arise,"[43] slide past one another at some plate boundaries, and converge (crash or crunch together) at others. The paper also provided other details about how plate tectonics works and made a compelling case for why the theory should be embraced by scientists.

After publication of their paper, Isacks, Oliver, and Sykes were hailed for how they had unified the various scientific discoveries into the plate tectonics theory. Because of this accomplishment, they came to be known as the founding fathers of plate tectonics. Today the theory they developed forms the basis for scientific understanding of how the earth works. "Their work," says geologist and seismologist Arthur L. Lerner-Lam, "was key in convincing scientists of the explanatory power of the 'new global tectonics,' and opened up new areas of research that even today remain fundamental."[44]

CHAPTER THREE

Many Layers of Mystery

I n the North Atlantic Ocean, just south of the Arctic Circle and east of Greenland, lies the island country of Iceland. World famous for spectacular scenery such as majestic cliffs, underwater canyons, a crystal-clear lake, hot springs, and geysers, Iceland draws several hundred thousand visitors each year. But scientists from all over the world are drawn to Iceland because of a different characteristic—one that is visible evidence of the plate tectonics theory. Slicing through the center of the country is the Mid-Atlantic Ridge, which serves as the boundary between the North American and Eurasian Plates. Iceland's Thingvellir National Park is the only place in the world where an oceanic ridge—which is so named because it is in the ocean depths—rises above the surface of the water. "You stand there, and you can imagine you're on the floor of the ocean,"[45] says Ken Verosub, who is a distinguished professor of geology at the University of California–Davis.

Ridges and Plates

Oceanic ridges are created when hot magma from deep within the earth moves upward to the surface and oozes out through gaps or cracks in the crust. The magma cools and solidifies, forming new crust; as this process continues over time, plates are pushed apart. "Picture two giant conveyor belts," says the USGS, "facing each other but slowly moving in opposite directions as they transport newly formed oceanic crust away from the ridge crest."[46] The Mid-Atlantic Ridge is part of the immense, planet-circling underwater chain of mountains known as the global mid-ocean ridge. Along with separating the Eurasian and North American Plates in the North Atlantic Ocean, the mid-ocean ridge forms the boundary between the African and South

American Plates in the South Atlantic. In the Pacific Ocean, the East Pacific Rise (which is part of the same oceanic global mountain chain) is in the South Pacific and serves as the boundary between six different plates.

Geologists have identified seven major plates: the African, Antarctic, Eurasian, North American, South American, Pacific, and Indo-Australian, the latter of which is sometimes considered two separate plates, the Australian and Indian. According to the Los Alamos National Laboratory's Earth and Environmental Sciences division, the Pacific Plate, which lies beneath the Pacific Ocean, is the largest of all the plates, spanning nearly 40 million square miles (104 million sq. km). In addition to the major plates, there are dozens of minor plates. One of the smallest is the Juan de Fuca, which is 250 miles (402 km) off the coast of Oregon and Washington and is bordered by the Pacific and North American Plates. Another minor plate, the Scotia Plate, is located in the Southern Hemisphere, tucked between the South American and Antarctic Plates. The tiniest of all the plates is the Galápagos Microplate, which covers 4,600 square miles (11,914 sq. km). It is beneath the Pacific Ocean off the west coast of South America, not far from the Galápagos Islands.

Some plates carry either continents or oceans, while most plates carry both. The USGS explains: "Most plates are part continental and part oceanic. Take the North American Plate, for example. Its western half is dominated by the North American continent, but its eastern half forms part of the Atlantic Ocean basin. In comparison, the Pacific Plate is essentially all oceanic." These and all other plates are constantly on the move, although they travel at different speeds. "The fastest plate races along at 15 centimeters (6 inches) per year," says the USGS, "while the slowest plates crawl at less than 2.5 centimeters (1 inch) per year."[47]

Geologists are able to measure the approximate speed of plate movement by studying ocean floor magnetic striping records. These records have shown that the Pacific, Nazca, and Cocos Plates are some of the world's fastest moving, whereas the African and Eurasian Plates are the slowest.

The mechanism that drives plate movement has been a topic of debate since the continental drift theory was proposed in the early

twentieth century. Alfred Wegener believed that the continents moved around the planet by plowing their way through the crust. He was unsure about the forces that propelled the continents, although he offered two possibilities: centrifugal force caused by the earth's rotation and tidal forces caused by the gravitational pull of the sun and moon. These theories were only speculation; Wegener himself expressed doubt that either was adequate for explaining how the continents were propelled across the earth. Before his death he wrote: "It is probable the complete solution of the problem of the forces will be a long time coming."[48]

Today scientists widely agree that plate movement is fueled by the great heat of the planet's interior. Many are convinced that the mechanism for plate movement is convection currents deep in earth's mantle, although precisely how this happens is still being researched and debated. "Much remains unknown," says geologist Tom Simkin, "particularly about the processes operating below the ever-shifting plates and the detailed geological history during all but the most recent stage of Earth's development."[49]

Types of Plate Boundaries

Tectonic plates come together at boundaries, of which there are three primary types: divergent, convergent, and transform. Where plates are moving apart from each other, such as those divided by the mid-ocean ridge, this is a divergent boundary. Yet these plates do not continue moving apart forever, as Washburn University geology professor Tambra L. Eifert explains: "If they did, our Earth would continue to grow larger throughout time. Once the oceanic plates move far enough away from the hot upwelling magma at the mid-ocean ridge, they cool off and sink beneath the weight of a continental plate or another oceanic plate."[50] In general, says Eifert, the heavier plate will sink beneath the lighter plate, which is a geological process known as subduction.

WORDS IN CONTEXT

subduction

The action of one plate being forced under another.

Subduction occurs at convergent plate boundaries, where two plates move toward each other and eventually collide (converge). "At these boundaries," says Eifert, "large sections of the plate subduct (descend) into the deeper mantle and are destroyed."[51] This type of tectonic activity caused the disappearance of an oceanic plate called Farallon—or at least it was believed to have disappeared. In March 2013 a team of geologists announced that they had found evidence that it had not been entirely lost. About 100 million years ago, the Farallon Plate was nestled between the converging Pacific and North American Plates. As the two enormous plates pushed and crunched against the Farallon Plate, it was forced beneath North America, where it sank into the mantle—but not all of it did. The new study found that large slabs of the Farallon Plate still exist about 62 miles (100 km) below California near the Sierra Nevada.

Where two continental plates converge, neither of them subducts. The collision causes rock to be thrust upward, which results in mountain building. According to the National Oceanic and Atmospheric Administration (NOAA), convergent plate movement created the immense jagged peaks of the Himalayan mountain range. An estimated 50 million years ago, the mountains began forming due to a collision between the Australian and Eurasian Plates. When the African and Eurasian Plates converged, this resulted in formation of the Mediterranean island of Cyprus.

Faults and Quakes

The third type of boundary, between two plates that slide horizontally past one another, is the transform boundary. It is also called

Thriving Life Between the Plates

The scientists who developed the plate tectonics theory predicted the existence of hydrothermal vents, which are hot springs in the deep ocean. They form when cracks develop in the ocean floor as a result of plate movement. Seawater flows into the cracks, is heated by magma, and then oozes out of the cracks and rises up to the seafloor. Scientists had been actively searching for such vents since the 1960s but were unable to locate any. That changed in February 1977 at a divergent plate boundary near the Galápagos Islands in the eastern Pacific Ocean.

A team of three scientists in a small vessel known as a submersible plunged 8,000 feet (2,438 m) below the surface of the water and became the first to locate hydrothermal vents—but that was not all they found. The warm, misty-blue water was teeming with life: species of crabs, clams, tube worms, and mussels that no one had ever seen before were clustered around the hot water flowing up from the cracks in the ocean floor. One of the scientists in the submersible, geologist Jack Corliss, was astonished by what he saw. Speaking by phone with a graduate student, he said, "Isn't the deep ocean supposed to be like a desert?" When the student answered yes, Corliss replied, "Well, there's all these animals down here." According to the NOAA, additional hydrothermal vents have since been found in many other locations where underwater volcanic processes are active.

Quoted in Cristina Luiggi, "Life on the Ocean Floor, 1977," *Scientist*, September 1, 2012. www.the -scientist.com.

the transform-fault boundary because it is the zone where faults are created. Faults are breaks in rock caused by heavy stress from the crunching, sliding plates. The size of faults varies widely, from no larger than a hair to hundreds of miles long. Two of the largest faults in the world are California's San Andreas Fault and the Anatolian Fault in Turkey, both of which are so enormous they are visible by astronauts in space. According to Nicholas van der Elst, a seismologist at Columbia University's Lamont-Doherty Earth Observatory in Palisades, New York, faults may be located most anywhere in the world. The largest, however, are in plate boundaries where plates continuously grind and scrape against each other. Faults are never stationary or static, as van der Elst explains: "Plate boundaries are always growing and changing, so these faults develop kinks and bends as they slide past each other, which generates more faults."[52]

WORDS IN CONTEXT

faults

Areas of fractured rock along plate boundaries that are caused by the stress of plate movement; most earthquakes occur in fault zones.

Because the biggest faults are located at plate boundaries, the risk of earthquakes is higher in these zones than in any other area. The quakes occur because the rocks in the crust have reached a certain limit and snapped, as science journalist and editor Maggie Koerth-Baker explains: "Faults can get stuck on one another and, over time, build up tension like a rubber band being pulled back. Earthquakes happen when the tension gets released and the pieces of the fault move suddenly with the pent-up force of many decades."[53]

Even though fault zones are the most common sites for earthquakes, they can also occur in areas located far away from faults. For example, intraplate earthquakes are those that strike in the middle of a plate, rather than at a boundary. In August 2011 an intraplate earthquake struck in central Virginia near the town of Mineral, which is deep in the interior of the North Atlantic Plate. The quake registered 5.8 on the Richter scale, which measures the magnitude of earthquakes on a scale from 1 to 10. Like all intraplate quakes, this one was puzzling to scientists. Boston College scientist Alan Kafka writes: "It is not surprising to seismologists that an earthquake would occur in

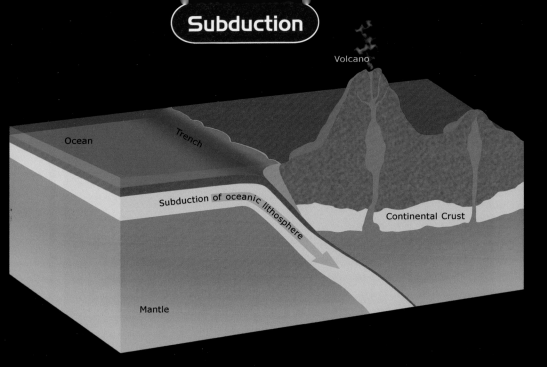

Subduction

The process of subduction results in the destruction of old oceanic crust. During the process of subduction tectonic plates collide. The collision forces one plate to descend beneath the other. In this diagram, plates of oceanic rock and continental rock collide, forcing the heavier oceanic rock to descend. This process leads to formation of an oceanic trench. It also produces intense friction between the two plates, which results in so much heat that the sinking rock melts. The melted oceanic plate may then rise upwards to form a volcano or it may melt back into the earth's mantle.

Virginia, but why it occurred at that particular location, at that particular time, and why it was a magnitude 5.8 remains a mystery."[54]

When major earthquakes strike, it can result in widespread devastation in terms of property loss, injuries, and death. But as tragic as these quakes are, they are quite rare. According to the USGS, each year an estimated 500,000 detectable earthquakes (meaning able to be measured with seismographic equipment) occur throughout the world. Of those, only about 20 percent are ever felt by humans, and just .02 percent cause damage.

The First Map of the Ocean Floor

One of the most famous maps of all time was created in 1977 by scientists Bruce C. Heezen and Marie Tharp. Known as the World Ocean Floor Map, it was the first depiction of the seafloor that had ever been developed. Prior to the publication of this map, scientists knew very little about what the seafloor looked like on a global scale, as geologist Evelyn Mervine explains: "Almost nothing was known about the topography of the seafloor." Heezen and Tharp's map was hailed not only for its remarkable accuracy but also for its aesthetic beauty; it was painted by Heinrich Berann, a renowned Austrian artist famous for his landscapes and panoramas. "Berann masterfully captured the dramatic mountain ranges of the mid-ocean ridges in his painting," says Mervine. She goes on to say that the World Ocean Floor Map was a revolutionary map for the worldview of oceanographers. "All of a sudden, oceanographers had an elegant, dramatic picture of the mid-ocean ridges running through the world's oceans like seams on a baseball. The map made sense in the framework of the young science of plate tectonics."

Evelyn Mervine, "A Famous Ocean Floor Map," *American Geophysical Union Blogosphere*, December 24, 2010. http://blogs.agu.org.

Volcanoes and Hot Spots

One area of the world where earthquakes are common is Indonesia. It is located in Southeast Asia and lies between the Indian and Pacific Oceans, part of a region called the Pacific Ring of Fire. Rather than a single landmass, Indonesia is a chain of thousands of islands known as an archipelago. The two largest islands are Sumatra and Java. According to the NOAA, the seafloor around Indonesia is among the most seismically active areas on earth. This is because of the country's location at the junction of the Eurasian, Pacific, Australian, and Philippine Plates. Says the USGS: "Frequent volcanic eruptions and frequent earthquake shocks testify to the active tectonic processes which are currently in progress in response to the continued movement of these major plates."[55] About 130 active volcanoes are located throughout Indonesia's islands, which is the most of any country in the world.

Volcanoes form in different sizes and shapes, with some resembling cones and others with a broad, flattened, dome-like shape (known as shield volcanoes). Like so many other geological phenomena, volcanoes exist solely because of plate tectonics. A Smithsonian National Museum of Natural History booklet explains:

> Vivid reminders that our planet is geologically active, volcanic eruptions are generated by the same heat engine that drives Earth's plates. Volcanoes form at places where large quantities of heat escape at the surface—sometimes quite dramatically. Earth's volcanoes vary widely in size, form, and explosivity. Some erupt violently, others pour out rivers of lava. This diversity is largely related to their plate-tectonic environments.[56]

Nearly all the world's volcanoes are located along, or very close to, plate boundaries. One notable exception is the Hawaiian Islands, which are the tops of enormous volcanic mountains. The Hawaiian Islands were formed entirely by volcanoes—but they are located in the middle of the Pacific Ocean more than 2,000 miles (3,219 km) from the nearest plate boundary. This is due to a phenomenon that geophysicist John Tuzo-Wilson introduced in 1963, which he called the hot spot theory. The USGS explains: "Wilson noted that in certain locations around the world, such as Hawaii, volcanism has been active for very long periods of time. This could only happen, he reasoned, if relatively small, long-lasting, and exceptionally hot regions—called *hotspots*—existed below the plates that would provide localized sources of high heat energy (*thermal plumes*) to sustain volcanism."[57]

In developing his theory, Wilson concluded that the distinctive shape of Hawaii's Emperor Seamounts (the chain of underwater mountains that forms the islands) had resulted by the Pacific Plate moving over a hot spot in the mantle, beneath what is now the island of Hawaii. "Heat from this hotspot produced a persistent source

WORDS IN CONTEXT

plate boundary

The place where two tectonic plates meet; the three primary types of plate boundaries are divergent, convergent, and transform.

of magma by partly melting the overriding Pacific Plate," says the USGS. "The magma, which is lighter than the surrounding solid rock, then rises through the mantle and crust to erupt onto the seafloor, forming an active seamount."[58] Over time, volcanic eruptions caused the seamounts to grow until they rose above the water to form island volcanoes. Continuous plate movement eventually carried the islands beyond the hot spots that had created them, cutting them off from their magma source, thus ending volcanism. "As one island volcano becomes extinct, another develops over the hotspot, and the cycle is repeated," says the USGS. "This process of volcano growth and death, over many millions of years, has left a long trail of volcanic islands and seamounts across the Pacific Ocean floor."[59]

WORDS IN CONTEXT

hot spots

Areas far from plate boundaries where volcanoes can occur.

The Ever-Changing Earth

Like the Hawaiian Islands, Iceland was also formed from volcanic activity, and it is another of the most seismically active places on earth. As a result, the country has been significantly changed by plate tectonics. Over the past ten thousand years, the Thingvellir Rift Valley's appearance has been radically changed by the spreading and sinking of the earth's crust at the plate boundary, as well as by earthquakes. Geologists estimate that the valley floor has widened 230 feet (70 m) and has sunk 131 feet (40 m).

Currently, at the Mid-Atlantic Ridge, the North American and Eurasian Plates are slowly pulling away from each other at a rate of about 1 inch (2.5 cm) per year. Sue Strickland of NASA's Earth Science division explains: "Not only is the mid-ocean ridge changing the geography of Iceland, it's also responsible for the volcanic activity which created the island. As the two tectonic plates shift, fissures periodically form in the crust. Over time, these gaps allow molten rock from underground to surface as lava, creating Iceland's many volcanoes."[60] According to Strickland, more than fifteen volcanoes have erupted in Iceland during the past century.

In late August 2014 one of Iceland's largest volcanoes, Bardarbunga, erupted, and it continued erupting over the following months. By mid-October 2014, says *National Geographic* science editor Devin Powell, the volcano had "spewed out enough molten rock so far to fill 740 Empire State buildings and has buried, on average, an area the size of an NFL football field every 5.5 minutes."[61] The volcano is located in a remote region of Iceland, far away from any populated areas, so no lives were in danger. Still, scientists have closely monitored the Bardarbunga eruption. What they learn by observing it will hopefully lead to a better understanding of ocean floor formation, which, Powell writes, "like Iceland's eruptions, takes place at geological seams where tectonic plates tear apart from each other."[62]

The Bardarbunga volcano, one of Iceland's largest, spews molten rock during eruptions that lasted for several months in 2014. Eruptions such as this present scientists with a chance to better understand the changes that continue to shape the earth.

Many regions throughout the world are changing because of plate tectonic activity that is fueled by earth's great heat. This has happened throughout the planet's history, and it continues to happen now. According to *National Geographic*:

> In much the same way that geographic borders have separated, collided, and been redrawn throughout human history, tectonic plate boundaries have diverged, converged, and reshaped the Earth throughout its geologic history. Today, science has shown that the surface of the Earth is in a constant state of change. We are able to observe and measure mountains rising and eroding, oceans expanding and shrinking, volcanoes erupting and earthquakes striking.[63]

Scientists have no doubt that as time goes by, these geological phenomena will continue, which means that earth will keep changing in innumerable ways.

CHAPTER FOUR

Protecting Human Life

In October 2012 seven prominent Italian earthquake experts were convicted of manslaughter and sentenced to six years in prison. They had been charged with failing to properly warn citizens and local government officials in the town of L'Aquila, Italy, about a major earthquake. On April 6, 2009, during the predawn hours, a 6.3 magnitude earthquake struck the mountainous province of Abruzzo and caused widespread death and destruction. More than three hundred people were killed, and at least fifteen hundred others were injured. The experts who were put on trial and convicted were not charged because they failed to predict the earthquake; even the prosecution acknowledged that such prediction was impossible. Rather, they were accused of negligence for ignoring the signs that a deadly quake was imminent. "One important point about L'Aquila," says USGS seismologist Susan E. Hough, "is that it really wasn't about 'failure to predict' an earthquake, but that officials went too far in telling people there was nothing to worry about—i.e., talking them out of their fears. There is a difference."[64]

For approximately six months prior to the devastating earthquake, the region had experienced intermittent tremors and small quakes that collectively are known as a seismic swarm. On some days this seismic activity shook the earth fifty times or more. The tremors were troubling enough that L'Aquila officials convened a meeting at the end of March 2009 to assess the situation and evaluate the risk. At that meeting, the experts downplayed the risk of a major earthquake. They urged citizens to remain calm, stating that

WORDS IN CONTEXT

seismic swarm

A series of tremors or small quakes that may or may not indicate that a major earthquake is going to strike.

the rumblings, though they were frequent some days, were not necessarily indicative that a large earthquake was imminent. Such a quake could not be deemed impossible, they said, but it was not likely. Many people living in the Abruzzo region interpreted that to mean there was no cause for alarm. "No one expected to be told the exact time of the quake," says Vincenzo Vittorini, a doctor whose wife and daughter were killed when their apartment building collapsed during the quake. "We just wanted to be warned that we were sitting on a bomb."[65]

Scientists Erupt

When the verdict and sentencing were announced, scientists throughout the world were shocked and angry. Many spoke out in support of the defendants, saying that the conviction could severely harm future seismology research. Two scientists who had served with the Italian government's disaster preparedness agency promptly resigned. The Italian National Institute of Geophysics and Volcanology publicly expressed its regret and concern over the verdict. More than five thousand members of the American Association for the Advancement of Science signed an open letter to Italy's president, Giorgio Napolitano, which stated: "The basis for those indictments appears to be that the scientists failed to alert the population of L'Aquila of an impending earthquake. However, there is no way they could have done that credibly. . . . There is no accepted scientific method for earthquake prediction that can be reliably used to warn citizens of an impending disaster."[66]

One of the experts who criticized the verdict was David Oglesby, who is an associate professor of earth sciences at the University of California–Riverside. According to Oglesby, to predict that a large earthquake is likely based on a "relatively commonplace sequence of small earthquakes and to advise the local population to flee" would constitute "both bad science and bad public policy." Oglesby went on to issue a stern warning about the dangerous precedent this type of verdict could set:

> If scientists can be held personally and legally responsible for situations where predictions don't pan out, then it will be very hard to find scientists [willing] to stick their necks out in the future. . . . I can understand the grief of people who lost loved

ones and the frustration that people feel when terrible events happen, especially ones outside their control. Convicting honest scientists of manslaughter does nothing to help this situation and may well put a chill on exactly the kind of science that could save lives in the future.[67]

In November 2014, after a series of appeals, the convictions were overturned for six of the defendants and the sentence reduced for the seventh. Scientists worldwide were relieved, with the National Institute of Geophysics and Volcanology president Stefano Gresta stating, "The

A seismograph records a major earthquake in Haiti in 2010. Scientists worldwide monitor seismic activity, but even with modern equipment they cannot accurately predict earthquakes. This issue lay at the heart of a court case following a deadly 2009 earthquake in L'Aquila, Italy.

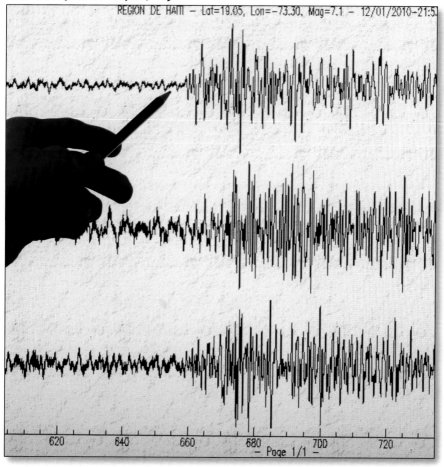

No Guarantees

Earthquakes, at present, cannot be predicted with any certainty. Yet there are ways to protect lives and property in the event of a major quake. Buildings, for instance, can be designed to withstand violent shaking without collapsing. In the United States the tallest structure in a seismic hot zone (earthquake-prone area) is the New Wilshire Grand in downtown Los Angeles. Scheduled for completion in 2017, the tall, slender hotel and office complex will be 1,100 feet (335 m) high. Protective features such as a thick concrete core, structural braces known as outriggers, and columns were incorporated in the design. All of these features can help keep the building erect in an earthquake.

Leonard Joseph is lead engineer on the New Wilshire Grand project. His primary responsibility is to make sure the skyscraper meets earthquake building standards. But Joseph, who has helped create skyscrapers in Malaysia, Taiwan, and China, is the first to say that it is impossible to guarantee that any building will stand up to the powerful force of an earthquake. "Earthquake design is a fuzzy proposition," he says. "You can't ask an engineer to guarantee that a building will never collapse in an earthquake. That is not fair, and that is not the deal that society has made with the construction world." Rather, says Joseph, engineers such as himself can ensure that buildings "behave as well as possible" in an earthquake. "Even that's a heavy responsibility," he says.

Quoted in Thomas Curwen, "Built to Defy Severe Quakes, the New Wilshire Grand Is Seismically Chic," *Los Angeles Times*, November 2, 2014. http://graphics.latimes.com.

credibility of Italy's entire scientific community has been restored."[68] Not everyone was overjoyed at the announcement, however. Citizens of L'Aquila and other nearby villages were stunned and angry, believing that justice was not done.

Unpredictability

Earthquake prediction is a future goal for seismologists everywhere. Most agree that today, however, it is virtually impossible to make accurate predictions about when and where quakes will strike. Hough says earthquake prediction remains extremely challenging. She explains that throughout the 1970s and 1980s, scientists were optimistic about their ability to predict major quakes; in fact, some experts publicly stated that such a capability was imminent. Today, says Hough, "the earthquake science community is older and wiser."[69] She says that for scientists to make the kind of accurate predictions the public wants would require being able to identify a reliable precursor. In other words, seismologists would need some kind of signal to indicate that a big quake is imminent. Such coveted warning signs are yet to be found, as Hough explains: "So far as we have been able to tell, the earth simply does not provide any observable signal to tell us a big quake is on the way."[70]

What scientists do know is where active earthquake zones are located throughout the world. For many, perhaps even most of those zones, scientists have been able to estimate the expected long-term average rates of earthquakes. Thus, they have a good idea of the highest- and lowest-hazard regions. "But," says Hough, "any active plate boundary is fair game for a big earthquake, any time." All in all, declaring that any one area of the planet will be the site of the next massive earthquake is neither prudent nor worthwhile, as Hough explains: "Take a map of the world's most active plate boundaries and throw a dart; where it lands is as good a guess as any. The only valid reason for imminent concern about any particular area is, oddly enough, right after a big earthquake has struck."[71]

Geophysicist Erik Klemetti is another earthquake expert who acknowledges the futility of accurately predicting earthquakes. He says a very popular topic related to earthquake prediction is pattern recognition. This is the practice of drawing conclusions about earthquakes based on patterns, such as solar activity or increases in quakes during certain phases of the moon. He writes: "In geology, there is probably no bigger a subject than 'pattern recognition' (or lack thereof) in earthquake prediction, to the point that some claim they can predict when and where an earthquake will strike. Sadly, we just can't do that with our current technology and knowledge of the Earth, but people still fall prey to believing in these false patterns."[72]

> **WORDS IN CONTEXT**
>
> *precursor*
>
> A reliable signal that would let scientists know a quake is going to strike.

Scientists know that earthquake occurrence is closely related to stresses on individual faults within the earth. According to Klemetti, however, it is not possible to fully explore that with today's technology. "Remember, the focus (hypocenter) of most earthquakes are at depths of tens to hundreds of kilometers below the surface," says Klemetti, "and we humans have only drilled into the uppermost few kilometers of the planet." He writes:

> Collecting data that can tell us the state of stress on all the known active faults alone is far beyond our current capabilities—and that is exactly what we need to be able to make accurate predictions of when an earthquake will occur on a given fault. . . . We haven't even come close to developing a reliable (and believable) method for predicting earthquakes. All of this adds up to this simple statement: prediction of earthquakes is currently impossible.[73]

Crucial Preparedness

In the absence of reliable earthquake prediction methods, remaining vigilant about earthquakes and being prepared for them is essential. Along coastal areas, it is equally crucial for citizens to be prepared for massive ocean waves known as tsunamis that can be spawned by underwater quakes. Hough says that preparedness remains the best defense against devastating earthquakes. As an example, she cites the 9.0 magnitude Tohoku-Oki earthquake that struck Japan on March 11, 2011. The earthquake and subsequent tsunami were catastrophic, killing more than fifteen thousand people. Yet, says Hough, "the disaster clearly would have been much worse without that country's decades of investment in preparedness—the stringent building codes, early warning systems, tsunami systems and citizen education."[74]

Japan is known for being better prepared for earthquakes than most any country on earth. One primary focus of preparedness is schools,

WORDS IN CONTEXT

tsunami

Massive, deadly ocean waves that are often spawned by underwater earthquakes.

Skyscrapers line the winding streets of Tokyo in Japan. Japan, a country that is prone to earthquakes, has some of the world's most stringent building codes to help prevent building collapses in an earthquake.

where Japanese students participate in earthquake drills every month. When the alarm sounds, children are taught to go under their desks headfirst and hold tight until they hear the all clear. Those playing outside are taught to rush to the center of any open spaces to avoid being hit by falling or flying debris. Stringent building regulations in Japan ensure that earthquake-proof features are built into all major structures. Skyscrapers, for instance, are constructed to sway during a quake to prevent collapse. To keep the public informed when an earthquake strikes, Japanese television and radio stations immediately switch to emergency broadcasts. Also, at the first sign of any magnitude quake, all trains in Japan stop on the tracks to prevent them from derailing.

One of the most important aspects of Japan's earthquake preparedness program is how the country involves its citizens and communicates with them. "In Japan, they have a civilization of earthquake preparedness," says Pedro Silva, a professor of civil and environmental engineering at George Washington University, who has visited Japan three times. "What really amazed me was that even at the kindergarten level, they receive earthquake briefings continuously. It's really in their culture."[75] Silva and a number of other experts are concerned that the United States has not embraced earthquake preparedness countrywide. San Francisco, for instance, is much more vigilant about earthquakes than many other cities. "The Northwest coast of the U.S., that's where the big problem is, if you ask me," says Silva. "The potential is there for a mega-earthquake of the magnitude we saw in Japan. You would be unlikely to see many buildings withstand it."[76]

Fiery Eruptions

As with earthquake prediction, volcanologists (scientists who specialize in volcanoes) cannot say precisely where and when volcanoes are going to erupt—but trying to identify potential eruptions is among their highest priorities. Geologist and climate scientist Bill McGuire writes: "With half a billion or so people now living in the danger zones surrounding the world's volcanoes, honing the ability to predict future eruptions and, thereby, save lives, is something of a Holy Grail for volcanologists."[77] In the absence of precise accuracy, McGuire says that volcanologists have an easier time predicting volcanic eruptions than seismologists who attempt to predict earthquakes. He explains why:

WORDS IN CONTEXT

volcanologist

A scientist who specializes in studying volcanoes.

> First, for molten magma to open a path to the surface it has to break rock. This results in swarms of small earthquakes that are readily detected by seismometers. Second, the magma must also make space for itself; shouldering the surrounding rock sideways and upwards, causing the ground surface to swell. This can also be detected using any one of a variety of monitoring techniques, including GPS; albeit a more sophisticated version than the one we frequently [use] in our cars.[78]

According to McGuire, one of the biggest challenges of volcanic eruption prediction is that no one knows exactly how many active volcanoes exist throughout the world. "We do know, however, that around 1,500 have erupted at some point during the past 10,000 years," he says, "and all have the potential to erupt again." McGuire estimates that there are an equal number of active volcanoes that have not erupted but have been lying dormant and could erupt at any time. "These are the really scary ones," he says, "as when it comes to volcanoes (all other things being equal), it is often the case that the longer the wait; the bigger the bang."[79]

One volcano being closely monitored in the United States is in Yellowstone National Park. It is known as the Yellowstone supervolcano because of its mammoth size and potential for destruction. Experts say that it is thousands of times more powerful than the average

Without Warning, a Mountain Explodes

Japan is known for keeping a close watch on seismic activity. With more than one hundred active volcanoes and a strong history of earthquakes, the country has invested heavily in the most sophisticated monitoring and warning devices. But on September 27, 2014, Japanese scientists were caught off guard when Mount Ontake erupted without warning. Several hundred hikers were on the enormous volcano when it suddenly exploded with a deafening boom, sending white plumes of smoke and ash billowing high into the air. Tons of ash rained down from the sky and blanketed the surrounding area, burying some people alive. The catastrophic event lasted for more than two hours, and by the time it was over, more than sixty people were dead.

Because Japan so closely monitors its volcanoes, many people wondered why the disastrous eruption was not detected earlier. According to Georgia Institute of Technology geophysicist Joe Dufek, the ability to make such predictions depends on the type of eruption. The one on Mount Ontake was what scientists call a phreatic eruption, which occurs when red-hot magma boils the groundwater around a volcano. This creates steam that continues to build up until it finally explodes. According to Dufek, phreatic eruptions are not detectable ahead of time with seismic equipment. "There's not a lot of lead time in this kind of eruption," he says. "The monitoring in Japan as a whole is probably the densest network anywhere in the world. If anyone could catch it, it would probably be these guys."

Quoted in Angela Fritz, "Lack of Warning in Japan's Mt. Ontake Volcano Eruption Raises Questions," *Capital Weather Gang* (blog), *Washington Post*, September 30, 2014. www.washingtonpost.com.

volcano. According to the USGS, there have been three "cataclysmic eruptions" of the Yellowstone volcano "more powerful than any in the world's recorded history." Together, the USGS adds, "the three catastrophic eruptions expelled enough ash and lava to fill the Grand Canyon."[80] One of these eruptions occurred 2.1 million years ago, another 1.3 million years ago, and the third at a relatively "recent" 640,000 years ago. The USGS says that the odds of a current eruption are extremely small: about one chance in one thousand.

Hope Through Research

With ongoing studies of volcanoes and earthquakes, as well as other geological phenomena, scientists continue to learn more about the effects of plate tectonics on the earth. For instance, after Japan's catastrophic 2011 earthquake, an international team of scientists embarked on a study to determine why it happened. Sixteen months after the quake struck, scientists on a deep-sea-drilling vessel called *Chikyu* drilled into a fault off the Japanese coast and installed special instruments that would measure its temperature. This would allow the group to determine how much energy was released during the earthquake to calculate the fault's friction, or how easily the rocks rubbed against each other.

To illustrate the concept of friction in an earthquake, Oregon State University geophysicist Robert Harris uses a skiing metaphor. "One way to look at the friction of these big blocks," says Harris, "is to compare them to cross-country skis on snow. At rest, the skis stick to the snow and it takes a certain amount of force to make them slide. Once you do, the ski's movement generates heat and it takes much less force to continue the movement. The same thing happens with an earthquake." After nine months of operation, the scientists had recorded temperatures from the fault zone—an extraordinarily deep 4.3 miles (6.9 km) below the surface of the water and 2,700 feet (823 m) below the ocean floor. "The project itself was an engineering feat and an amazing one at that," says Harris. "It pushed the limits of that technology as far as they can go."[81]

Through data gathered by the instruments, the scientists learned that the fault was exceptionally slippery, and this contributed to the severity of the earthquake. Another related characteristic was that the area was found to be the thinnest fault zone on earth, which was

The friction that occurs when tectonic plates rub against each other during an earthquake is similar to the action of cross-country skis on snow. The skis require a certain amount of force to make them slide but once that movement generates its own heat, less force is needed to keep them going.

also a contributing factor in the earthquake's magnitude. "This is data that we've never had before," says Harris. "It will be helpful in understanding the dynamics of earthquakes in the future." As exciting as the study findings were, however, Harris and his fellow scientists acknowledge that it is only the beginning of all that they need to learn. "There is still a lot we don't yet know."[82]

There is certainly much that remains unknown, and in the coming years, as research continues, scientists hope to remedy that. Geologists, seismologists, volcanologists, and other experts will keep pursuing research to learn more about the mighty forces of plate tectonics and how these forces affect the planet. In the process, this will hopefully save human lives. "The most exciting developments in any science are often the ones that nobody imagined until someone stumbled across something," says Hough. "That might be the best part about science: not the discoveries you think are right around the corner, but the discoveries that *are* right around the corner that you don't know about yet."[83]

CHAPTER FIVE

Plate Tectonics and Global Climate

Through decades of research, scientists have gained a wealth of knowledge about plate tectonics and what it means for the planet. In the process, they have learned about the close relationship between plate movement and earth's changing climate. Specifically, they have come to understand how the continuous shaping and reshaping of the crust over tens of millions of years has resulted in significant climatic variations. According to British scientist Mark Maslin, one area of the world where plate movement has caused a radical shift in the climate is East Africa. Maslin says this climate shift has profoundly changed the landscape of the region, as he explains: "The extraordinary forces of plate tectonics and a changing climate have transformed East Africa from a relatively flat, forested region to a mountainous fragmented landscape dominated by the rapid appearance and disappearance of huge, deep-water lakes."[84]

Africa is just one example of a region where climatic changes have resulted from plate tectonics; similar changes have occurred all over the world. Studying these variations helps scientists better predict how climate is likely to change in the future, which in turn enables them to determine how this will affect humans and other living things. The NOAA writes:

> Climatic variability, including changes in the frequency of extreme events (like droughts, floods and storms), has always had a large impact on humans. A particularly severe El Niño, or relatively short drought, can cost US citizens billions of dollars. For this reason, scientists study past climatic variability on various time scales to gain clues that will help society plan for future climate change.[85]

Mountain Building and Climate

Profound changes in climate are directly related to the worldwide distribution of earth's vast mountain ranges. As these geological wonders have built up and changed over millions of years, this has resulted in associated shifts in global climate, largely due to air circulation in the atmosphere. Pennsylvania State University scientist Eric J. Barron says that in its simplest form, this influence can be compared to that of a large rock in a stream. "The rock acts as a barrier to the flow of the fluid," says Barron, "and the current pattern is modified around and downstream from the barrier." He continues:

> The positions of the continents and oceans (causing differences in heating) and the distribution of regions of high topography control the position of the large-scale waves in the atmosphere, such as the jet stream, and therefore control the pattern of the weather. A change in topography may well control the distribution of cold air masses or the track of winter storms. Such changes could initiate glaciation in a particular region by promoting even greater cooling, or they could warm high-latitude regions, which may otherwise be cool.[86]

Residents of northern Bolivia make their way through flooded streets in 2007. An El Niño event that year caused heavy rains and flooding in some parts of the world and extreme heat in other areas. Scientists are trying to better understand the relationship between plate tectonics and climate change.

Central Asia's massive Tibetan Plateau is an example of how mountain ranges have dramatically affected climate. The largest and tallest plateau in the world, the Tibetan Plateau covers more than 965,000 square miles (2.5 million sq km) and stretches through three countries: Tibet, China, and India. It is a sprawling landscape of glaciers, alpine lakes, and waterfalls, and serves as one of the largest storehouses of freshwater on the planet. The plateau is ringed by mountains, including the towering Himalayas to the south. Scientists have long believed that the Tibetan Plateau started to form approximately 50 million years ago when the two large India and Eurasia landmasses collided and thrust upward. According to Maslin, the plateau's effect on the regional climate has been truly amazing. Dur-

How Earthquakes Can Affect Climate

It is widely known that volcano eruptions can profoundly affect climate because they emit carbon dioxide (CO_2), ash, and sulfuric gases into the atmosphere. Earthquakes can also contribute to climate shifts, as German and Swiss scientists discovered in a study published in July 2013. During a research expedition in the northern Arabian Sea, the scientists found evidence that methane gas (a major component of natural gas) had surged up through the seafloor. Follow-up studies revealed that a major earthquake had occurred close to that location in 1945. The team concluded that the gas had escaped after the quake caused fractures in the seafloor where pockets of natural methane were stored. The scientists estimated that 261 million cubic feet (7.4 million cu. m) of methane had broken loose as a result of the quake-induced fracture in the seafloor.

This finding was important because along with CO_2 and water vapor, methane is a powerful heat-trapping gas. Together, these gases help stabilize earth's climate by contributing to a phenomenon known as the greenhouse effect. It has long been known that methane is produced during the decomposition of plant or other organic compounds, as well as being a by-product of agriculture. Now, scientists are aware that methane can also end up in the atmosphere due to earthquakes. This will likely be a source of future research in the study of climate change.

ing the summer months, he likens it to a "huge heat engine, absorbing solar energy which it transfers to the atmosphere, causing immense convection currents. With all this hot air rising, air is sucked in from all round, including moist air from the Indian Ocean that produces intense Southeast Asian monsoons."[87]

Another highly visible result of how plate movement has influenced climate is in the African country of Ethiopia, where an enormous rift (fracture in the crust) formed. "This rifting," says Maslin, "was caused by a hotspot of magma under northern East Africa heating the crust [and] causing it to split down the middle like an overdone apple pie."[88] Maslin goes on to explain that the rift's formation created a deep, wide valley (known as the Great Rift Valley) with mountains up to 2 miles (3.2 km) high on either side. According to Maslin, the effect of this valley formation on the local climate was dramatic. "The East Rift's mountains prevented moist air from the Indian Ocean from passing over East Africa," he says, "causing the region to dry even further. The topography . . . completely changed from a homogenous flat region covered in moist forest, to a mountainous landscape with plateaus and deep rift valleys, where vegetation varied from cloud forest to desert scrub."[89]

How Oceans Influence Climate

The same plate movement that has shaped, molded, and changed earth's landscape over millions of years has also changed the oceans. This, in turn, has profoundly affected the global climate. Scientists have long known that the oceans play a crucial role in climate regulation, and now they also know that this is intertwined with plate tectonic activity. Referring to the "complex interplay among the continents, oceans, and atmosphere," scientists Gerald H. Haug and Lloyd D. Keigwin write: "Like pieces of a puzzle, Earth's moving tectonic plates have rearranged themselves on the surface of the globe—shifting the configurations of intervening oceans, altering ocean circulation, and causing changes in climate."[90]

One way the world's vast oceans influence global climate is their ability to store immense amounts of heat from the sun. In fact, the oceans can store far more heat than land can hold. The Global Development Research Center (GDRC) explains: "Because it is a fluid, the ocean diffuses the effects of a temperature change for great distances via vertical mixing and convective movements. The solid land cannot, so the sun's heat penetrates only the thin, upper crust." The GDRC goes on to explain that one consequence of the ocean's ability to absorb such a large amount of heat is that when an area of ocean becomes warmer or cooler than usual, "it takes much longer for that area to revert to 'normal' than it would for a land area. This also explains why 'maritime' climates tend to be less extreme than 'continental' ones, with smaller day-night and winter-summer differences."[91]

Powerful currents, which collectively move the ocean's water around the globe like a giant conveyor belt, play a crucial role in climate regulation. "Surface currents are largely wind-driven," says the GDRC, "although the rotation of the earth, the presence of continents, and the oceans' internal dynamics also have a strong influence." The primary way oceanic currents influence the climate is by transporting heat, as the GDRC explains: "Horizontal currents, particularly those moving north or south, can carry warmed or cooled water as far as several thousand kilometres. The displaced water can then warm or cool the air and, indirectly, the land over which this air blows."[92] One example of this is a swift-moving ocean current known as the Gulf Stream. From its point of origin in the warm, tropical waters of southern Florida, the Gulf Stream moves north through the Atlantic Ocean, acting as the main conveyor of heat. The GDRC says that the Gulf Stream "bathes the shores of Western Europe, producing a climate that is surprisingly mild for that latitude."[93]

Closely related to currents are oceanic phenomena called upwellings, which also influence climate. Upwellings form when winds blowing across the ocean surface push water away and deep, colder water wells up from below and rises toward the surface to replace it. According to NASA, upwelling lowers sea surface temperatures and increases the frequency of summertime fog along the northern and central California coast. Thick fog develops when relatively cold surface water chills and saturates the humid air above it.

WORDS IN CONTEXT

upwelling

An oceanic phenomenon that forms when winds blowing across the ocean surface push water away and deep, colder water rises toward the surface to replace it.

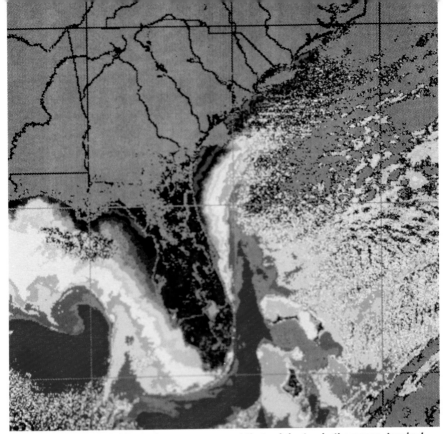

The Gulf Stream, a swift-moving ocean current that originates in the warm, tropical waters of southern Florida (pictured), acts as a conveyor of heat as it moves north through the Atlantic Ocean. The Gulf Stream helps regulate climate in many parts of the world.

Volcanic Eruptions and Global Climate

Among the most dramatic geological phenomena to influence global climate are the world's volcanoes. Powerful eruptions can send massive clouds of rock, ash, and gases high into the atmosphere. One of these gases is carbon dioxide, or CO_2. Along with water vapor, methane, and other "heat-trapping" gases, CO_2 helps stabilize earth's climate by contributing to a phenomenon known as the greenhouse effect. Karen Harpp, a geology professor at Colgate University in Hamilton, New York, describes the greenhouse effect as "a type of insulation around the planet" that is caused by gases that trap the sun's heat after it has radiated off the surface of the earth. "The greenhouse effect is essential for our survival," says Harpp, "because it maintains the temperature of our planet within a habitable range."[94] She estimates that 110 million tons (99.8 million metric tons) of CO_2 are emitted into the atmosphere each year by the eruption of volcanoes throughout the world.

As prolific as CO_2 is after a major volcanic eruption, most scientists agree that the resultant atmospheric haze has a much more intense effect on climate. According to Harpp, large eruptions inject ash particles and sulfur-rich gases into the troposphere and stratosphere, which are upper layers of the atmosphere. "The small ash particles decrease the amount of sunlight reaching the surface of the earth and lower average global temperatures," says Harpp. "The sulfurous gases combine with water in the atmosphere to form acidic aerosols that also absorb incoming solar radiation and scatter it back out into space."[95] Harpp goes on to explain that ash and aerosol clouds from massive volcano eruptions can spread through the atmosphere quickly, circling the entire planet within weeks of an eruption.

WORDS IN CONTEXT

atmospheric haze

The cloud of ash and sulfur-rich gases that forms after a volcano eruption and can result in widespread cooling.

One of the most notable examples of rapid movement of a volcanic cloud occurred after the August 26, 1883, eruption of the Indonesian volcano known as Krakatau. The eruption was cataclysmic, creating a towering column of ash nearly 25 miles (40 km) high. "Darkness immediately enveloped the neighboring Indonesian islands of Java and Sumatra," says Harpp. "Fine particles, however, rode atmospheric currents westward. By the afternoon of August 28th, haze from the Krakatau eruption had reached South Africa and by September 9th it had circled the globe, only to do so several more times before settling out of the atmosphere."[96]

For many years scientists believed that the ash clouds from volcanoes were the primary force behind global temperature alteration after an eruption. According to Harpp, that view began to change after the 1982 eruption of a volcano in Mexico known as El Chichón. Investigators found that the bigger culprit was emissions of sulfur-rich gases known as sulfur dioxide. "Only two years earlier, the major Mt. St. Helens eruption had lowered global temperatures by about 0.1 degree C," says Harpp. "The much smaller eruption of El Chichón, in contrast, had three to five times the global cooling effect worldwide."[97] Scientists discovered that even though El Chichón had a much smaller ash cloud than Mount Saint Helens, it emitted more than forty times the volume of sulfur dioxide.

According to the UCAR Center for Science Education, it is now widely known that sulfur dioxide is much more effective at cooling global climate than volcanic ash particles. The gas moves into the stratosphere, where it combines with water to form sulfuric acid aerosols. The center explains: "The sulfuric acid makes a haze of tiny droplets in the stratosphere that reflects incoming solar radiation, causing cooling of the Earth's surface. The aerosols can stay in the stratosphere for up to three years, moved around by winds and causing significant cooling worldwide. Eventually, the droplets grow large enough to fall to Earth."[98]

A Worldwide Climate Changer

Most scientists believe that of all the volcano eruptions in history, none has affected global climate as dramatically as the April 1815

Climate Change Moving Plates?

For many years scientists have known that the movement of tectonic plates can significantly influence climate over time. But in April 2011 a team of geologists released a study that found the reverse to be true: Long-term climate change has the potential to move earth's plates. Led by Australian National University researcher Giampiero Iaffaldano, the team used computer models to match up known monsoon patterns with plate movement. The team found that the Indian Plate movement has accelerated by about 20 percent over the past 10 million years. Says Iaffaldano:

> The significance of this finding lies in recognising for the first time that long-term climate changes have the potential to act as a force and influence the motion of tectonic plates. It is known that certain geologic events caused by plate motions—for example the drift of continents, the closure of ocean basins and the building of large mountain belts— have the ability to influence climate patterns over a period of a million years. Now we know that the opposite holds as well: long-term climate change, or the natural changes in climate patterns over millions of years, can modify the motion of plates in a feedback mechanism.

Quoted in PhysOrg, "Monsoons Spinning the Earth's Plates: Study," April 13, 2011. http://phys.org.

eruption of Mount Tambora. Located on the remote Indonesian island of Sumbawa, Tambora's catastrophic eruption occurred after thousands of years of lying dormant. The eruption propelled massive amounts of ash and volcanic gases into the atmosphere, blocking out sunlight and resulting in widespread, significant global cooling. In a *Smithsonian* magazine article about Tambora's eruption, journalist Robert Evans refers to it as the "most destructive explosion on earth in the past 10,000 years." He writes:

> Three columns of fire shot from the mountain, and a plume of smoke and gas reached 25 miles into the atmosphere. Fire-generated winds uprooted trees. Pyroclastic flows, or incandescent ash, poured down the slopes at more than 100 miles an hour, destroying everything in their paths and boiling and hissing into the sea 25 miles away. . . . The ground shook, sending tsunamis racing across the Java Sea. An estimated 10,000 of the island's inhabitants died instantly.[99]

Ash continued to fall from the sky for weeks after the volcano had quieted down. Sources of fresh water, which were already in short supply, became contaminated, while cropland was ruined and forests were destroyed. An estimated 90,000 people on Sumbawa and the neighboring island of Lombok died as a result of the Mount Tambora eruption—and the volcano's devastating effects traveled far beyond Indonesia. "Great quantities of sulfurous gas from the volcano mixed with water vapor in the air," says Evans. "Propelled by stratospheric winds, a haze of sulfuric acid aerosol, ash and dust circled the earth and blocked sunlight."[100] In China and Tibet, unseasonably cold weather killed trees and rice crops, while any surviving crops were destroyed by flooding. Countries throughout Europe, particularly Spain, suffered severe hardship because of global cooling. Thus, 1816 became known as "the year without summer."[101] Although Tambora's eruption took place thousands of miles from the United States, the country was not spared from its terrible aftermath. The New England region was hit especially hard, with blinding snowstorms sweeping through the East Coast in June 1816 and hard frost continuing into late summer. This severe weather caused the shortest growing season ever recorded in

Volcanic ash blankets the Indonesian city of Yogyakarta after a volcanic eruption in 2014. Scientists say that volcanic ash in the atmosphere has an intense effect on climate.

the region, with nearly all crops being completely destroyed. "Failing crops and rising prices in 1815 and 1816 threatened American farmers," says Evans. "Odd as it may seem, the settling of the American heartland was apparently shaped by the eruption of a volcano 10,000 miles away. Thousands left New England for what they hoped would be a more hospitable climate west of the Ohio River."[102]

Changing Planet, Changing Climate

Plate tectonics offers a scientific explanation for how the land and oceans have formed and changed over time, as well as the effects on global climate. Because the earth is a restless planet and plates are never still, these changes are continuous—meaning that generations from now, the earth and climate may be very different from what people are accustomed to today.

SOURCE NOTES

Introduction: A Restless Earth

1. Quoted in Patrick Hughes, "Alfred Wegener (1880–1930)," NASA Earth Observatory. http://earthobservatory.nasa.gov.
2. Richard Conniff, "When Continental Drift Was Considered Pseudoscience," *Smithsonian*, June 2012. www.smithsonianmag.com.
3. Quoted in James Lawrence Powell, *Mysteries of Terra Firma: The Age and Evolution of the Earth*. New York: Free Press, 2001, p. 92.
4. Quoted in Alfred Wegener Institute, "The Copernicus of Geosciences," 2011. www.awi.de.
5. Francis J. Pettijohn, "Rollin Thomas Chamberlin: 1881–1948," National Academy of Sciences, 1970. www.nasonline.org.
6. Adam T. Mansur, "Not Continental Drift but Plate Tectonics," ProQuest Discovery Guides, May 2010. www.csa.com.
7. Roy Livermore, "Plate Tectonics: In Memory of Britain's Greatest Rock Stars," *Telegraph* (London), September 3, 2013. www.telegraph.co.uk.

Chapter One: Early Scientific Beliefs

8. Jacquelyne Kious and Robert I. Tilling, *This Dynamic Earth: The Story of Plate Tectonics*. Washington, DC: US Geological Survey, 2014. http://pubs.usgs.gov.
9. Marcel van den Broecke, "Facts and Speculations on Production and Survival of Ortelius' 'Theatrum Orbis Terrarum' and Its Maps," Artwis.com, September 1, 1986. www.artwis.com.
10. Quoted in Prasenjit Duara, Viren Murthy, and Andrew Sartori, eds., *A Companion to Global Historical Thought*. West Sussex, UK: Wiley, 2014, p. 155.
11. Naomi Oreskes, ed., *Plate Tectonics: An Insider's History of the Modern Theory of the Earth*. Cambridge, MA: Westview, 2001, p. 4.
12. Allan Krill, *Not Getting the Drift: A Hard Look at the Early History of Plate-Tectonic Ideas*, 2014. http://folk.ntnu.no.

13. Samuel Warren Carey, *Theories of the Earth and Universe: A History of Dogma in the Earth Sciences*. Stanford, CA: Stanford University Press, 1988, pp. 90–91.

14. John R. Gribbin, *Planet Earth*. Oxford: Oneworld, 1988. Kindle edition.

15. Oreskes, *Plate Tectonics*, p. 4.

16. Oreskes, *Plate Tectonics*, p. 4.

17. Michael J. Smith and John B. Southard, "Exploring the Evolution of Plate Tectonics," National Science Teachers Association, August 31, 2001. www.nsta.org.

18. Smith and Southard, "Exploring the Evolution of Plate Tectonics."

19. Smith and Southard, "Exploring the Evolution of Plate Tectonics."

20. Quoted in Naomi Oreskes, *The Rejection of Continental Drift: Theory and Method in American Earth Science*. New York: Oxford University Press, 1999, p. 48.

21. Oreskes, *The Rejection of Continental Drift*, p. 17.

22. Mansur, "Not Continental Drift but Plate Tectonics."

23. Mansur, "Not Continental Drift but Plate Tectonics."

24. Gribbin, *Planet Earth*.

25. Andrew Gleadow, "The Day the Earth Moved," *Cosmos*, December 16, 2013. https://cosmosmagazine.com.

26. Gleadow, "The Day the Earth Moved."

27. Hughes, "Alfred Wegener (1880–1930)."

Chapter Two: Development of the Plate Tectonics Theory

28. Gordon J.F. MacDonald, "How Mobile Is the Earth?," in Oreskes, *Plate Tectonics*, p. 113.

29. MacDonald, "How Mobile Is the Earth?," p. 115.

30. Edmond A. Mathez, ed., *Earth Inside and Out*. New York: New Press, 2000. Excerpted at American Museum of Natural History. www.amnh.org.

31. Kious and Tilling, *This Dynamic Earth*.

32. Kenneth R. Lang, "Third Rock from the Sun—Restless Earth," NASA's Cosmos, 2010. http://ase.tufts.edu.

33. Mathez, *Earth Inside and Out*.

34. Kious and Tilling, *This Dynamic Earth*.
35. H.H. Hess, "History of Ocean Basins," *Petrologic Studies*, November 1962. www.mantleplumes.org.
36. J.I. Merritt, "Hess's Geological Revolution," *Best of PAW: 1946–1966*, September 24, 1979. www.princeton.edu.
37. Gleadow, "The Day the Earth Moved."
38. Merritt, "Hess's Geological Revolution."
39. Frederick J. Vine, "Reversals of Fortune," in Oreskes, *Plate Tectonics*, p. 46.
40. Gleadow, "The Day the Earth Moved."
41. Kenneth Chang, "Quakes, Tectonic and Theoretical," *New York Times*, January 16, 2011. www.nytimes.com.
42. Quoted in Chang, "Quakes, Tectonic and Theoretical."
43. Bryan Isacks, Jack Oliver, and Lynn R. Sykes, "Seismology and the New Global Tectonics," *Journal of Geophysical Research*, September 15, 1968. www.mantleplumes.org.
44. Quoted in Columbia University Earth Institute, "John Oliver, a Father of Plate Tectonics, Dies," January 7, 2011. www.earth.columbia.edu.

Chapter Three: Many Layers of Mystery

45. Quoted in Andrea Mustain, "Iceland Offers Rare Glimpse of Tectonic Meeting Place," Live Science, June 21, 2012. http://m.livescience.com.
46. US Geological Survey, "Understanding Plate Motions," September 15, 2014. http://pubs.usgs.gov.
47. US Geological Survey, "Putting the Pieces Together," October 3, 2014. http://geomaps.wr.usgs.gov.
48. Quoted in Hughes, "Alfred Wegener (1880–1930)."
49. Tom Simkin et al., "This Dynamic Planet," US Geological Survey, 2006. http://pubs.usgs.gov.
50. Tambra L. Eifert, "Tectonic Plates," Geology for Today, 2013. www.geology4today.com.
51. Eifert, "Tectonic Plates."
52. Quoted in Becky Oskin, "Fault Lines: Facts About Cracks in the Earth," Live Science, September 25, 2014. www.livescience.com.

53. Maggie Koerth-Baker, "Climate Change and Earthquakes: It's Complicated," *Boing Boing* (blog), August 4, 2011. http://boing boing.net.

54. Alan Kafka, "The Enigma of Why a Magnitude 5.8 Earthquake Occurred in Virginia," *Musings on Earthquakes and Related Matters* (blog), December 27, 2011. https://akafka.wordpress.com.

55. US Geological Survey, "Indonesia," March 3, 2014. http://earth quake.usgs.gov.

56. Smithsonian National Museum of Natural History, *Plate Tectonics and Volcanoes*. www.mnh.si.edu.

57. US Geological Survey, "'Hotspots': Mantle Thermal Plumes," May 5, 1999. http://pubs.usgs.gov.

58. US Geological Survey, "'Hotspots.'"

59. US Geological Survey, "'Hotspots.'"

60. Sue Strickland, "Mid-Atlantic Ridge in Iceland," *Earth Science Picture of the Day* (blog), August 17, 2010. http://epod.usra.edu.

61. Devin Powell, "Icelandic Eruption Spews Record-Breaking Amounts of Lava, with No Signs of Slowing," *National Geographic*, October 14, 2014. http://news.nationalgeographic.com.

62. Powell, "Icelandic Eruption Spews Record-Breaking Amounts of Lava, with No Signs of Slowing."

63. *National Geographic*, "Plate Tectonics." http://education.national geographic.com.

Chapter Four: Protecting Human Life

64. Susan E. Hough, interview with author, December 20, 2014.

65. Quoted in BBC News, "Italy Scientists on Trial over L'Aquila Earthquake," September 20, 2011. www.bbc.com.

66. Quoted in Jennifer Welsh, "Italian Earthquake Researchers Sentenced to Six Years in Prison," *Business Insider*, October 22, 2012. www.businessinsider.com.

67. Quoted in Jethro Mullen, "Italian Scientists Resign over L'Aquila Quake Verdicts," CNN, October 23, 2012. www.cnn.com.

68. Quoted in BBC News, "L'Aquila Quake: Scientists See Convictions Overturned," November 10, 2014. www.bbc.com.

69. Susan E. Hough, "Why Can't We Predict the Next Big Quake?," CNN, March 21, 2011. www.cnn.com.

70. Hough, "Why Can't We Predict the Next Big Quake?"

71. Hough, "Why Can't We Predict the Next Big Quake?"

72. Erik Klemetti, "Earthquakes, Patterns and Predictions," *Eruptions* (blog), *Wired*, May 30, 2013. www.wired.com.

73. Klemetti, "Earthquakes, Patterns and Predictions."

74. Hough, "Why Can't We Predict the Next Big Quake?"

75. Quoted in Alan Greenblatt, "Japanese Preparedness Likely Saved Thousands," NPR, March 13, 2011. www.npr.org.

76. Quoted in Greenblatt, "Japanese Preparedness Likely Saved Thousands."

77. Bill McGuire, "Life in the Volcanic Danger Zone: How Well Can Scientists Predict Eruptions?," *Guardian* (London), September 29, 2014. www.theguardian.com.

78. McGuire, "Life in the Volcanic Danger Zone."

79. McGuire, "Life in the Volcanic Danger Zone."

80. US Geological Survey, "Questions About Yellowstone Volcanic History," July 6, 2012. http://volcanoes.usgs.gov.

81. Quoted in Oregon State University, "Scientists Calculate Friction of Japan's 9.0 Earthquake in 2011," news release, December 5, 2013. http://oregonstate.edu.

82. Quoted in Oregon State University, "Scientists Calculate Friction of Japan's 9.0 Earthquake in 2011."

83. Hough, interview.

Chapter Five: Plate Tectonics and Global Climate

84. Mark Maslin, "How Climate Change and Plate Tectonics Shaped Human Evolution," *Scientific American*, November 14, 2013. www.scientificamerican.com.

85. National Oceanic and Atmospheric Administration, "Introduction to Paleoclimatology," July 16, 2002. www.ncdc.noaa.gov.

86. Eric J. Barron, "Climatic Variation in Earth History," Understanding Global Climate Change: Earth Science and Human Impacts, 1994. www.ucar.edu/communications/gcip/m10histclim var/m10htmlshort.html.

87. Maslin, "How Climate Change and Plate Tectonics Shaped Human Evolution."

88. Maslin, "How Climate Change and Plate Tectonics Shaped Human Evolution."

89. Maslin, "How Climate Change and Plate Tectonics Shaped Human Evolution."

90. Gerald H. Haug and Lloyd D. Keigwin, "How the Isthmus of Panama Put Ice in the Arctic," *Oceanus*, 2004. www.whoi.edu.

91. Global Development Research Center, "How the Oceans Influence Climate." www.gdrc.org.

92. Global Development Research Center, "How the Oceans Influence Climate."

93. Global Development Research Center, "How the Oceans Influence Climate."

94. Karen Harpp, "How Do Volcanoes Affect World Climate?," *Scientific American*, October 4, 2005. www.scientificamerican.com.

95. Harpp, "How Do Volcanoes Affect World Climate?"

96. Harpp, "How Do Volcanoes Affect World Climate?"

97. Harpp, "How Do Volcanoes Affect World Climate?"

98. UCAR Center for Science Education, "How Volcanoes Influence Climate," 2015. http://scied.ucar.edu.

99. Robert Evans, "Blast from the Past," *Smithsonian*, July 2002. www.smithsonianmag.com.

100. Evans, "Blast from the Past."

101. William K. Klingaman and Nicholas P. Klingaman, *The Year Without Summer: 1816*. New York: St. Martin's, 2013.

102. Evans, "Blast from the Past."

IMPORTANT PEOPLE IN THE HISTORY OF PLATE TECTONICS

Samuel Warren Carey: An Australian geologist who was a leading proponent of the expanding earth theory.

Bruce C. Heezen and Marie Tharp: Research conducted by Heezen, a geologist, and Tharp, an oceanographer and cartographer, contributed to the scientific understanding of seafloor spreading; together they created and published the world's first scientific map of the seafloor, the World Ocean Floor Map, in 1977.

Harry H. Hess: A Princeton University geologist who in 1960 theorized that the movement of continents resulted from newly formed ocean crust spreading away from mid-ocean ridges, which came to be known as seafloor spreading.

Arthur Holmes: A British geologist who expanded on the continental drift theory by suggesting that the movement of continents is caused by mantle convection, meaning the slow, steady flow of heat from earth's interior to the surface.

Bryan Isacks, Jack Oliver, and Lynn R. Sykes: Columbia University geologists who published a landmark paper in 1968 in which they theorized that earth's crust is broken into a number of plates (oceanic and continental) that are constantly in motion.

Matthew F. Maury: A scientist who, as a lieutenant with the US Navy during the mid-1800s, discovered the first evidence of underwater mountains in the central Atlantic Ocean using an underwater mapping technique known as bathymetry.

Dan Peter McKenzie and Robert L. Parker: Geologists who in 1967 published the first scientific paper describing the principles of plate tectonics: that the surface of the earth is broken into major and minor plates. To illustrate that the plates are constantly moving, McKenzie and Parker drew comparisons with enormous icebergs.

Abraham Ortelius: A Flemish geographer and mapmaker who observed in the late sixteenth century that the Americas looked as though they had been "torn away" from Europe and Africa.

Harry Fielding Reid: A Johns Hopkins University geologist who published a report in the early 1900s in which he described how stored energy is released and spread during an earthquake, a theory he calls elastic rebound.

Antonio Snider-Pellegrini: An Italian American geographer who suggested that the reason for identical tropical plant fossils being discovered in North America and Europe was that the continents may have once been connected.

Frank B. Taylor: An American geologist who in 1908 proposed that the long, curved mountain belts of Asia and Europe resulted from tidal forces of the moon pushing and pulling earth's crust, forming carpet-like folds.

John Tuzo-Wilson: A Canadian geophysicist who in 1965 coined the term *plate* in reference to the massive slabs of rock that make up earth's crust. It was also Tuzo-Wilson who discovered transform faults, as well as developed the hot spot theory to explain why active volcanoes may be located hundreds of miles away from plate boundaries.

Frederick J. Vine and Drummond Matthews: British geologists whose early 1960s studies of mid-ocean ridges and seafloor spreading were important contributions to development of the plate tectonics theory.

Alfred Wegener: A German meteorologist who developed the theory of continental drift, which was a monumental accomplishment and the predecessor to the plate tectonics theory.

FOR FURTHER RESEARCH

Books

John Dvorak, *Earthquake Storms: The Fascinating History and Volatile Future of the San Andreas Fault*. New York: Pegasus, 2014.

Wolfgang Frisch, Martin Meschede, and Ronald Blakey, *Plate Tectonics: Continental Drift and Mountain Building*. New York: Springer, 2011.

Robert M. Hazen, *The Story of Earth: The First 4.5 Billion Years, from Stardust to Living Planet*. New York: Penguin, 2012.

Craig Saunders, *What Is the Theory of Plate Tectonics?* New York: Crabtree, 2011.

Alicia M. Spooner, *Geology for Dummies*. Hoboken, NJ: Wiley, 2011.

John Wilson, *Ghost Mountains and Vanished Oceans*. Toronto, ON: Key Porter, 2011. Kindle edition.

Internet Sources

Carrie Arnold, "Rare Earthquakes Within Tectonic Plates Are Highly Deadly," *Discover*, August 29, 2013. http://discovermagazine.com/2013/oct/03-a-new-take-on-quakes.

Richard Conniff, "When Continental Drift Was Considered Pseudoscience," *Smithsonian*, June 2012. www.smithsonianmag.com/science-nature/when-continental-drift-was-considered-pseudoscience-90353214/?all&no-ist.

Andrew Gleadow, "The Day the Earth Moved," *Cosmos*, December 16, 2013. https://cosmosmagazine.com/earth-sciences/day-earth-moved.

Jacquelyne Kious and Robert I. Tilling, *This Dynamic Earth: The Story of Plate Tectonics*. Washington, DC: US Geological Survey, 2014. http://pubs.usgs.gov/gip/dynamic/dynamic.html.

Flora Lichtman and Sharon Shattuck, "Animated Life: Pangaea," *New York Times*, February 17, 2015. www.nytimes.com/2015/02/17/opinion/animated-life-pangaea.html.

Naomi Lubick, "Tiny Minerals May Have Shaped Earth's First Plate Boundaries," *Science News*, April 6, 2014. www.sciencenews.org/article/tiny-minerals-may-have-shaped-earths-first-plate-boundaries?mode=magazine&context=188465.

Smithsonian National Museum of Natural History, "Plate Tectonics and Volcanoes." www.mnh.si.edu/earth/text/4_0_0.html.

Thomas Sumner, "Plate Tectonics Spotted on Europa," *Science News*, September 8, 2014. www.sciencenews.org/article/plate-tectonics-spotted-europa?mode=magazine&context=189135.

John Weier, "Putting Earthquakes in Their Place: A New Map of Global Tectonic Activity," NASA Earth Observatory. http://earthobservatory.nasa.gov/Features/Tectonics.

Websites

Earth Science Concepts, National Park Service (www.nature.nps.gov/geology/education/concepts/concepts_platetectonics.cfm). This site explains the concept of plate tectonics in a variety of ways, including learning activities, articles, reports, and graphics.

Plate Tectonics, National Geographic Education (http://education.nationalgeographic.com/education/topics/plate-tectonics/?ar_a=1). This site provides a good collection of information about plate tectonics, with articles about oceanic ridges and trenches, major and minor plates, volcanoes, faults, and other related geological phenomena.

Plate Tectonics, Windows to the Universe (www.windows2universe.org/earth/interior/plate_tectonics.html). This information-packed site offers articles on topics such as why plates move, earth's history, myths and facts, volcanoes, and earthquakes, as well as links to current news articles.

US Geological Survey (www.usgs.gov). A wealth of information about plate tectonics is available through the site of the USGS, which is the United States' leading earth sciences agency.

INDEX